CONTENTS

Helion & Company Limited
Unit 8 Amherst Business Centre
Budbrooke Road
Warwick
CV34 5WE
England
Tel. 01926 499 619
Fax 0121 711 4075
Email: info@helion.co.uk
Website: www.helion.co.uk
Twitter: @helionbooks
Visit our blog http://blog.helion.co.uk/

Designed & typeset by Farr out Publications, Wokingham, Berkshire
Cover design by Paul Hewitt, Battlefield Design (www.battlefield-design.co.uk)
Printed by Henry Ling Ltd., Dorchester, Dorset

ISBN 978-1-912390-59-5

British Library Cataloguing-in-Publication Data
A catalogue record for this book is available from the British Library

We always welcome receiving book proposals from prospective authors.

Note: In order to simplify the use of this book, all names, locations and geographic designations are as provided in *The Times World Atlas*, or other traditionally accepted major sources of reference, as of the time of described events. Correspondingly, the term 'Congo' designates the area of the former Belgian colony of the Congo Free State, granted independence as the Democratic Republic of the Congo in June 1960 and in use until 1971 when the country was renamed Republic of Zaire, which, in turn, reverted to Democratic Republic of the Congo in 1997, and which remains in use today. As such, Congo is not to be mistaken for the former French colony of Middle Congo (Moyen Congo), officially named the Republic of the Congo on its independence in August 1960, also known as Congo-Brazzaville.

Citation to the 2nd Regiment of the Foreign Legion for the Completion of the Operation 'Leopard'

This is an excellent regiment which, since its creation in 1948, has never stopped providing its best service for France, wherever it was required to support her national interests. Its availability and military value enabled it to save, on 19 May 1978, French and other European civilians taken hostage, and to achieve complete success.

On 19 May 1978, an airborne operation for protection and rescue of the population of Kolwezi was conducted under difficult circumstances. Operating 6,000 kilometres from its base, under the energetic leadership of its commander, Colonel Erulin, this unit secured the region within less than 48 hours, saving lives of several hundred people, including French families.

With its courageous and effective action, in best tradition of airborne troops and the Foreign Legion, combining an unprecedented humanitarian mission with exemplary military action, the Foreign Legion of Paratroopers once again deserved the recognition of armed forces and the nation.

ABBREVIATIONS

4WD Four-wheel drive
AA anti-aircraft
AB Air Base
AB Agusta-Bell (Italian manufacturer of helicopters)
AdA Armée de l'Air (French Air Force)
AK Russian for Automat Kalashnikova; general designation for a class of Soviet or former East Block-manufactured class of assault rifles
AML Automitrailleuse Légère (general designation for a class of French-manufactured (Panhard) wheeled scout cars and armoured vehicles
An Antonov (the design bureau led by Oleg Antonov)
ANC Armée Nationale Congolaise, Congolese National Army (1960-1971)
APC Armoured Personnel Carrier
ATGM anti-tank guided missile
CAS Close Air Support
CASA Construcciones Aeronáuticas SA (Spanish aircraft manufacturer)
CBU cluster bomb unit
CIA Central Intelligence Agency (USA)
c/n construction number
CO Commanding Officer
COTAM Commandement du transport aérien militaire (Military Air Transport Command of the French Air Force, 1962-1994)
DGSE Direction Générale de la Sécurité Extérieure (Directorate-General for External Security; French external intelligence agency operating under the direction of the French Ministry of Defence)
DITRAC Division des Troupes Aéroportées Renforcées de Choc (Reinforced Airborne Shock-Troops Division, Congo/Zaire)
DRC Democratic Republic of the Congo (Congo-Kinshasa, also Zaire)
DoD Department of Defence (USA)
EAF Egyptian Air Force (official title since 1972)
ECM Electronic countermeasures
ELINT Electronic intelligence
ERV Escadron de Ravitaillement en Vol (Air Refuelling Squadron)
FAPLA Forcas Armadas Populares de Libertação de Angola (People's Armed Forces of Liberation of Angola; armed wing of the MPLA and then the official designation of the Angolan military, 1975-1992)
FAZ Forces Armées Zaïroise (Zairian Army, 1971-1996)
FAZA Force Aérienne Zaïroise (Zairian Air Force, 1971-1996)
FLEC Frente para a Libertação do Enclave de Cabinda (Front for the Liberation of the Enclave of Cabinda, Angola)
FNLA Frente Nacional de Libertação de Angola (National Front for the Liberation of Angola, armed group opposing Portuguese rule in Angola in 1960-1975, later fighting against MPLA government in the 1970s and 1980s)
FNLC Front National pour la Libération du Congo (National Front for the Liberation of the Congo)
HQ headquarters
IAP International Airport
IDF Israeli Defence Force
IDF/AF Israeli Defence Force/Air Force
IR Infra-red, electromagnetic radiation longer than deepest red light sensed as heat
Il Ilyushin (the design bureau led by Sergey Vladimirovich Ilyushin, also known as OKB-39)
IP Instructor Pilot
Km kilometre
LRAC Lance-Roquettes Anti Char (de 89mm modéle F1) (anti-tank rocket launcher calibre 89mm, model F1)
MANPADS man-portable air defence system(s) – light surface-to-air missile system that can be carried and deployed in combat by a single soldier
MBT Main Battle Tank
MHz Megahertz, millions of cycles per second
Mi Mil (Soviet/Russian helicopter designer and manufacturer)
MIA missing in action
MiG Mikoyan i Gurevich (the design bureau led by Artyom Ivanovich Mikoyan and Mikhail Iosifovich Gurevich, also known as OKB-155 or MMZ' "Zenit")
MILAN Missile d'infanterie léger antichar (French-made ATGM)
MoD Ministry of Defence
MPLA Movimento Popular de Libertaçâo de Angola (People's Movement for the Liberation of Angola, leftist anti-colonial movement in Angola of the 1960s and 1970s; later ruling party of Angola,

	1970s-2000s)
MPR	Mouvement populaire de la Révoultion (Popular Movement of the Revolution, Mobutu's political party)
NCO	Non-commissioned officer
OAU	Organisation of African Unity
ORBAT	Order of Battle
PMC	private military company
RAF	Royal Air Force (of the United Kingdom)
REC	Régiment Etranger de Cavalerie (Cavalry Regiment of the Foreign Legion)
REP	Régiment Etranger Parachutistes (Parachute Regiment of the Foreign Legion)
RHC	Régiment d'Hélicoptères de Combat (Combat Helicopter Regiment)
RIAOM	Régiment Interarmes d'Outre-Mer (Overseas Interarms Regiment)
RICM	Régiment d'Infanterie Chars de Marine (Marine Infantry Tank Regiment)
RIMa	Régiment d'Infanterie de Marine (Marine Infantry Regiment)
SARM	Service d'Action et de Renseignement Militaire (Zairian Military Intelligence Bureau)
SDECE	Service de Documentation Extérieure et de Contre Espionnage (Foreign Intelligence and Counterespionage Service in France), in 1982 re-organized as DGSE
SNIP	Service National d'Intelligence et Protection (National Service for Intelligence and Protection, top Zairian intelligence agency)
UNHCR	UN High Commissioner for Refugees
UNITA	Uniao Nacional para a Independência Total de Angola (National Union for the Total Independence of Angola, armed group opposing Portuguese Colonial rule in the 1960s and 1970s, then opposing MPLA until 2003)
UNRWA	United Nations Relief and Works Agency
USAF	United States Air Force
USD	United States Dollar (also US$)

CHAPTER 1
INTRODUCTION

In 1977, it appeared as if all of Africa was in a state of war. All sorts of armed conflicts – ranging from multiple anti-colonial insurgencies to all-out conventional wars – were raging almost everywhere, from Western Sahara in the north-west to Eritrea and Ogaden in the east, and from Libya and Chad in the north, to Angola and Rhodesia in the south, to name only a few. The former Belgian colony of the Congo, re-named Zaire in 1971, was no exception: a true labyrinth of diverse geopolitical factors, including ethnic, political and economic relations, caused an entire series of armed uprisings and insurgencies that raged ever since the country achieved independence in 1960. Indeed, the so-called 'Katangese Gendarmes', supported by the Angolan government, crossed the border to attack their former home, the province of Katanga, 'Africanised' into 'Shaba', in 1971. Their invasions resulted in two 'mini-secession attempts', also known as the Shaba Wars, fought in 1977 and 1978.

I started my studies of what is also known as the 'Kolwezi campaign' about ten years ago. Western interventions in reaction to the invasions of the 'Katangese Gendarmes' – a force never actually officially named that way – and the resulting Operations *Leopard* and *Red Bean*, were intensively researched and widely publicised in the French-language media. While saving and evacuating over 2,000 Europeans, the 2nd Parachute Regiment of the Foreign Legion (*2e Régiment Etranger Parachutistes*, 2e REP) suffered a loss of 5 killed and 20 wounded. In return, between 150 and 250 insurgents died in the course of an operation marked by the speed and determination of its execution, but also was conducted over 6,000 kilometres away from regiment's base. Furthermore, and in cooperation with Belgian Para Commandos, the 2e REP brought the crisis area under its control within only 48 hours, and kept it safe until it was relieved by an inter-African force composed of contingents from Morocco, Senegal, Togo and Gabon.

However, with most researchers concentrating on the brilliant rapid deployment of the French Foreign Legion to rescue hostages in the Kolwezi area, a comprehensive account of these affairs – one providing the 'big picture' – remained evasive. The research for my two articles on this topic, published in 2015, eventually formed the nucleus for this very book. The Kolwezi campaign of May 1978 effectively neutralized the independence movement of Katanga, directly linked to the spoiled secession of this area attempted in the period 1960-1963. Certainly enough, the secessionist movement did survive this crushing defeat, but it never recovered its former power.

The Heart of Africa

Although often neglected in various military studies, local terrain and climatic circumstances continue to dictate even modern warfare. Similarly, wars do not 'just happen', they are not fought in vacuum, on their own, but take place within very specific contexts. Correspondingly, studying them always requires taking a closer look at their geo-political, historical, and economic backgrounds.

What is nowadays the Democratic Republic of the Congo is the second largest state in Africa (after Algeria). It is four times the size of France or comparable in size to either the entirety of Western Europe, or to the United States east of the Mississippi River. Situated in central Africa, the country encompasses a vast depression, constituting its central area, and surrounding plateaus and mountains, all covered with dense vegetation. The area is practically encircled by the powerful Congo River – the second longest river in Africa and the seventh longest in the world – and also by the many other rivers of the Congo Basin. Formed on the Katanga Plateau in south-eastern Congo, it flows north and is navigable as far as the city of Kisingani, where a series of wide cataracts known as the Stanley Falls impedes navigation. Downstream from this point, the river is navigable again and arcs west, then south to Kinshasa (formerly Leopoldville), forming much of the boundary to the Central African Republic. The Congo River and its tributaries provide a vast

Most of the Congolese landscape is dominated by meandering rivers and rolling hills, usually covered by dense vegetation. (Mark Lepko Collection)

network of navigable waterways and have great – yet little used – hydroelectric potential: hydroelectric plants produce virtually all of the energy the country needs.

In its lower course, the Congo widens to form a lake, Pool Malebo, on the southern side of which is the capital Kinshasa, while Brazzaville, capital of the neighbouring Republic of the Congo, sits on the northern bank. Even more water can be found in the east of the Congo, where a number of lakes important for transportation and fishing mark much of its borders: Lake Albert and Lake Edward on the border to Uganda, Lake Kivu shared with Rwanda, the Lake Tanganyika – the seventh largest in the world – the border to Tanzania, and Lake Mweru straddles the Zambian border. The area along these lakes is dominated by the Ruwenzori Range, in the north-east – which contains Congo's highest point, Margherita Peak (5,109m/16,762ft) – while in the east there are the Virunga Mountains that include eight active volcanoes. The southern part of the country is dominated by dry grasslands interspersed with trees, fringed by the rugged Katanga Plateau, about 1,000m above the sea level.

The country's climate is very hot and humid, with an average annual temperature in the low central area about 27°C (80°F), and reaching peaks well above 40° during February, the hottest month. Frequent heavy rains occur from April to November north of the equator, and from October through May south of the equator.

A Blessing and a Course: Natural Resources

Congo is immensely rich in natural resources, and boasts some of the largest mineral deposits in the world.

According to various estimates, the county should have up to US$24 Trillion worth of untapped deposits of raw mineral ores. These include the world's largest reserves of cobalt and columbite-tantalite (better known as 'coltan', an ore containing two metals, niobium and tantalum), some of the largest reserves of diamonds, gold, silver, copper, uranium, tin, tungsten, zinc, manganese, and cadmium. Gold was found by the Belgians in the Kilo-Moto area in 1906, followed by copper, cobalt and uranium, discovered between 1911 and 1932; and no fewer than 82 specific minerals – foremost different heavy metals, much sought-after by modern high-technology industries – were found and described for the first time in the Congo. Congolese uranium was used in the nuclear bombs the USA dropped on Japan in 1945, while its massive coltan reserves are crucial for world-wide production of everyday electronic devices, like cell phones. Offshore oil reserves have been drilled since the mid-1970s, and some exploitation has taken place, but according to various estimates, untapped reserves are likely to further increase the potential income of the country in the future.

The worked mineral deposits are distributed over Precambrian massifs bordering, to the south, east and north-east, a vast sedimentary central basin. Most of the minerals are present in such quantities – and are so easily accessible – that they can be mined with little capital investment. Although theoretically state-controlled, much of the mining is done by small-scale artisanal miners who operate illegally. Counter clockwise, from south to north, the area around Mbuji-May in south-central Congo is the heartland of the country's diamond-mining industry, and mainly produces industrial diamonds. Additional diamantiferous exploitations are run in Tshikapa. The largest copper deposits are found in Tshiniama and Lubi, but copper is also found in southern Katanga, which is also rich in cobalt and uranium, and these are mined in Kolwezi, Likasi, Kambowe, Shinkolobwe, and Lubumbashi. Wolfram is mined in Bengo-Biri, while Katanga also contains huge mines for zinc, copper and germanium (mined in Kipushi), tin granite (Mitwaba), and the stanniferous pegmatite (mined in Manono). As of 1977, the country exported about 450,000 tonnes of copper, 51,000 tonnes of zinc, 10,200 tonnes of cobalt (60% of world production), 246 tonnes of cadmium, 85 tonnes of silver, and 112 kilograms of gold – nearly all of this from mines in the areas of Kolwezi and Lubumbashi, in the southern province of Katanga.[1]

Although declining since the 1990s, mining continues to account for almost 90% of Congolese export earnings. The major reason for the decreasing income is that most of the extraction is done in small and unregulated operations, next to no refining is undertaken inside the country, and there is next to no regulation of environmental impacts. Under such conditions, the central government always earned what was actually only a minimum in profits from extraction and exports.

In addition to being rich in mineral resources, Congo is also very rich in diverse vegetation. The country's forest reserves, covering 60% of the land, are considered the most extensive in Africa. Most of the northern part of Congo is covered with dense rain forest; and various rubber trees, coffee, cotton, oil palms, banana, coconut palms and plantain are widespread – although deforestation, caused by forestry and clearing for agriculture, is an increasing environmental problem, especially in the Bas-Congo region and around Kinshasa.

Downtown Kinshasa as seen in the early 1970s. (Mark Lepko Collection)

Population

The extreme climatic conditions prevalent in the Congo have limited settlement and development to areas along rivers and at high altitudes, many of which remained isolated until recently. The population consists of more than 200 ethnic groups, some 80% of which are Bantu-speaking people who migrated to the area from the northwest, beginning around 300 BC. During four centuries of slave trade the Portuguese alone claimed over 13.2 million lives from people living in the areas that are today in Congo. Nowadays, the largest single ethnic groups are the Lunda, Luba, Kuba, Bakongo (Kongo), Mongo, Mangbetu, and Azande. Pygmy groups are scattered throughout the rain forest zone, while a small number of people of European descent can be primarily found in major cities. French is the official language and principal business language, but more than 200 languages are spoken around the country, of which four are principal: Ligala along the Congo River, Kikongo between Kinshasa and the Coast, Swahili in the East, and Tshiluba in the south. Some 72% of the Congolese are nominally Christians, primarily – Roman Catholics – who account for about 52% of the total population. The majority of the rest adhere to traditional African beliefs, but syncretic sects, which combine practices of different religions – like Kimbanguism, which fuses Christian and traditional elements – have significant numbers of adherents.

The present population of about 62 million people is concentrated in the eastern highlands and along the, and only about 30% live in the cities. It consists of members of more than 170 diverse tribes, speaking nearly as many languages and dialects. The southern province of Katanga is populated by almost 30 additional tribes, grouped into three traditional 'empires': the Lundas, the Balubas, and the Bayekes. Nearly all of these speak Swahili, and for this reason the local population appears quite homogenous to outsiders. However, many within the Lunda and the Bayeke tribes long to restore the ancient kingdom of Katanga as it was before the colonial period.[2]

Other than the capital and the largest city, Kinshasa, major urban areas include the copper mining city of Lubumbashi (formerly Elisabethville); the south-central diamond-mining centre of Mbuji-Mayi (formerly Bakwanga); the south-eastern industrial city of Kolwezi; and the north-eastern Congo River port of Kisingani (formerly Stanleyville). The principal seaport is Matadi, positioned on the Congo estuary, relatively close to the stretch of the Atlantic coast measuring only 37km long, which forms the western border of the country.

Apart from South Africa, the Belgian Congo used to be the most industrialized and 'developed' country on the continent: as of 1958, 35% of the all adults were in salaried employment – a proportion unknown elsewhere in Africa. Certainly enough, only a few thousands of people in question were 'professionals': the majority of the Congolese worked as unqualified workers, farm labourers, petty clerks, artisans and repairmen: the Belgian paternalistic system needed 'disciplined semi-qualified drones', and not people that could take responsibilities, and thus in 1960 there were only 17 university graduates within the native population of over 20 million. The situation only gradually improved through the 1970s, because the government did very little for public education, and this remained dependent on schools founded by European and American missionaries. Officially, primary education was (and remains) compulsory, but only around 40% of school-age children attend school, while attendance at secondary schools is still only 18% of those of eligible age. At the present time, there are only four universities in the Congo, including two in Kinshasa, and a small number of teacher-training colleges and technical institutes.

Due to endemic corruption, nepotism, inexperience and general neglect over the last 50 years, much of the infrastructure developed by Belgian colonial authorities in the first half of the 20th Century deteriorated beyond any acceptable levels, and the economy has been severely distorted. Indeed, in the first 40 years of the Congolese independence, not a single road, rail-road, hospital or school has been built. The few infrastructure projects – primarily related to airports – that were completed served exclusively mining operations, bypassing the towns and villages, or servicing the needs of local despots: the once fertile farming areas were laid to waste, producing barely enough food for those working the land. Many parts of the country are not only destabilized but have been practically cut off from the outside world for decades.

Premature Independence of the Congo

The region that is nowadays within the borders of the Democratic Republic of the Congo was first united as the Congo Free State, a colony created by Belgian King Leopold II, in the late 19th Century, and during the infamous Berlin Conference of 1888, in particular. Indeed, the area and the people living there were for all practical reasons and purpose considered Leopold II's personal property. In 1908, the Belgians drastically reformed the area as their colony of Belgian Congo, and replaced their sadistic policies with one of paternalism. Within a few years, native workers on the plantations and in the newly developed mines in Katanga – many of them literally imported from such Belgian overseas possessions as Rwanda and Burundi – began enjoying better wages and living conditions than most workers in other African countries, while the educational and medical systems were put under the authority of the Roman Catholic Church. Still, the administration of the Belgian Congo, all of its public and technical services, were exclusively run by Europeans: even as of 1958, very few positions of executive or operational responsibility were held by the natives, while the first and only university in the entire territory was established only two years later. Unsurprisingly, out of a population of about 13,500,000 in 1959 no more than 10,000 Congolese were attending secondary or vocational training schools. By 1960, after 80 years of Belgian rule, there were exactly 17 native graduates with an education in Europe.[3]

Despite intentional under-education by the Belgians, the Congolese began organizing political movements and demanding independence during the 1950s. Correspondingly, municipal elections were held in 1957 in the three largest cities, marking the emergence of political parties – mostly created along tribal and language lines – which had previously been banned.[4] Eventually, pressure from them, but also that from multiple powers from abroad, forced the Belgians into another sudden change of mind: on 30 June 1960, they granted the territory independence as the Democratic Republic of the Congo (DRC).

Expected to bring relief from brutal, oppressive and racist Belgian rule, the independence took place in a great rush, before the nascent nation could develop its own administrative capabilities. Ever since, Congo has been nominally ruled by an entire series of governments that proved unable to exercise effective control. In a situation were there was an incredible lack of trained leaders and administrators, and other professionals necessary to exercise authority and manage the country, the nation became endemically plagued by ethnic rivalry, political instability, poverty, high crime rates, inadequate health-care, high incidents of tropical diseases – and armed conflicts.

At the time the DRC achieved independence, over 100 different political parties were existent, virtually all of these based upon ethnic and tribal groups. The first government was headed by President Joseph Kasa-Vubu (from the Abako branch of the Bakongo Tribe) and Prime Minister Patrice Lumumba (educated in theology and philosophy and fluent in French, Swahili and Lingala): while the former was the head of state, the latter was far better known and enjoyed far more popular support, but was also much more ambitious. While actually an uncompromising anti-imperialist, Lumumba was declared a 'leftist' by most Western governments (and the USA in particular), and then killed in an affair that saw a neck-deep involvement of the Central Intelligence Agency (CIA), in January 1961. Meanwhile – indeed: just a few hours after its declaration of independence – the new government faced a crisis that threatened its very survival, when the 25,000-strong Army of the Congo (Armée Nationale Congolaise, ANC) mutinied, demanding the ousting of its Belgian officers and pay increases for the enlisted men. Before long, the ANC was joined by many civilians that expected to inherit all Belgian possessions. As the lawlessness spread over major cities, thousands of European colonists fled in panic. Unable to request Belgian help for fear of enflaming the conflict, the government proved unable to enforce its authority and restore order.

The growing disorder was exploited by the leader of the Katanga province (the wealthiest part of the country), Moïse Kapenda Tshombe (who enjoyed Belgian support), to declare secession – only eleven days after the Congo obtained independence. This declaration was followed by a similar separation of the Kasai province led by Albert Kaolndji, a few weeks later. Belgium reacted by deploying its troops to Katanga, supposedly with the intention of restoring order and pace. However, a few days later their army marched into Elisabethville, the capital, and then into Leopoldville, provoking firefights with elements of the ANC and native civilians. Thus began eight years of political and armed unrest, and the terrible ravages of internal revolts, foreign interventions, and utmost turmoil, the origin of much of which was a dispute for the top command of the ANC between two Congolese non-commissioned officers (NCOs) – both prematurely advanced to the ranks of Major-general and Colonel: Victor Lundula and Joseph Désiré Mobutu, respectively.

Katangan Secession

A shrewd and ruthless politician, Tshombe declared his action as an attempt to salvage the mineral-rich area from the chaos that engulfed the rest of the country. No doubt, he was quick in securing support from abroad, foremost from the Belgian-owned *Union Minière* company, but also from private investors in the USA. Indeed, the Belgians rapidly helped consolidate the Katangan secession. On Tshombe's request, they quickly recruited, and flew into Katanga, a force of about 200 foreign mercenaries with the aim of not only reassuring fearful and beleaguered expatriates, upon whom local mining operations – and thus the prosperity of Katanga and the Congo – depended, but also in helping keep the province separated from the rest of the DRC.

The mercenaries arrived around the same time as a group of about 250 regular officers and NCOs of the Belgian Army, led by Major Crèvecoeur, contracted to create a Katangan Army based upon Belgian junior officers and NCOs. Combined, their efforts resulted in the establishment of a military totalling nearly 13,000 men, with about 400 – foremost Belgians, but also South African and Rhodesians, a few Frenchmen and some British – mercenaries of the *Compagnie Internationale* acting as an 'élite' spearhead.[5]

The Katangese military was in action before long. In March 1961, Katanga was threatened by a penetration in the north by some 400 Lumumbists who captured Manono. While the Katangan troops repelled this invasion, it was the mercenaries that recaptured the town. However, the foreigners were not ready to confront the 20,000-strong UN peace-keeping force, which meanwhile deployed in the DRC with the intention of stabilising the country. After pressure was applied upon their original governments, most were repatriated: by September 1961, at least 273 mercenaries had left and a further 65 were about to go. Left on its own, much of

Moise Tshombe during pre-independence negotiations in 1960. (Mark Lepko Collection)

the nascent Katangan military – meanwhile about 18,000 strong – melted away: most of its troops returned home, some were integrated into the armed forces of the Congo, but about 8,000 left for Angola. Tshombe's rule over Katanga thus ended after only two-and-a-half years, and his independence movement was crushed by the United Nations.

Mercenary Wars

Almost as soon as the UN contingents were withdrawn from the country, the northeast Congo erupted into tribal warfare, in 1964, resulting in some of the worst atrocities on the African continent ever. Supported by arms manufactured in the former Union of Soviet Socialist Republics (USSR, also 'Soviet Union'), and the People's Republic of China (PRC), and provided via the neighbouring – and 'Socialist'-controlled – Congo-Brazzaville, this uprising was widely perceived as 'pro-Communist' by much of the 'free World'. Correspondingly, and in a 'typically African' twist of fate, Tshombe was recalled from exile in Spain to take over as a prime minister in Kinshasa. Facing the crisis in the northeast, he reacted in his 'usual' fashion: by recruiting about 250 mercenaries from abroad, foremost from South Africa. Furthermore, he managed to return over 4,000 former members of the Katangese military from exile: about 1,600 of them were recruited into the ANC and organized into one 'commando' regiment of four battalions. Led by Major (promoted to Lieutenant-Colonel in January 1965) Mike Hoare, and followed by the Katangese, the mercenaries successively recaptured Mahagi, Aru, Aba, Faradje, and Watsa, and eventually sealed the border to Sudan. Indeed, in April 1965, Hoare declared the war as finished, and then turned his attention to Bondo, which fell on 30 May. By the time the last pockets of resistance had died out, some 35 mercenaries and hundreds of insurgents were dead.

Tshombe with one of the white mercenaries recruited to fight for an independent Katanga. (FNLC release)

Jean Schramme: A Mercenary or a Katangan Military Commander?

Many of the mercenary commanders involved in the Congo of the 1960s became something of a legend in their own life time. With a handful of exceptions, not one of them was of African origin: they became involved out of commercial interests and because soldiering was 'what they were good at'. One exception was Jean Schramme, also known as 'The Leopard'.

Born in Bruges, in Belgium, on 25 March 1929, he emigrated to the Congo in 1947, and become the owner of a plantation. During the 1950s, Schramme skilfully developed his business while becoming renowned as dealing fairly and without racism with his native employees: he learned Swahili, one of the local languages and adopted three local babies. When the Congo achieved independence, in 1960, Schramme decided to remain in the county and continue his business. Amid the growing chaos and disorder during the following years, he recruited a private militia composed of Belgians, a few French, some South Africans, a few Italians, and many locals, known as the 'Leopard Battalion', and was assigned the honorary rank of a Colonel in the Katangan military. In 1967, Schramme and his militia – together with Bob Denard – became involved in the Tshombe's plot for a coup against Mobutu. This ended in a disaster, forcing him, about 120 expatriate mercenaries and 600 Katangan Army troops to withdraw into the Stanleyville area, in eastern Congo. Pursued by the ANC, they retreated to the town of Bukavu, on the border of Rwanda. It was in this area that Schramme and his men held out against attacks by the ANC forces, at least ten times their number, for three months starting in August 1967. He gave up only once his men ran out of ammunition – and then withdrew into Rwanda. In April 1968, Schramme returned to Belgium but was almost instantly indicted for the murder of a white farmer in Katanga, and sentenced to 20 years in prison. However, already during this process he had been granted permission to emigrate to Brazil: because he was meanwhile married to a Brazilian citizen, he could not be extradited. Thus, he remained in Brazil until his death in 1988.

A still from a documentary movie, showing Jean 'The Leopard' Schramme. (Mark Lepko Collection)

Hardly was this crisis over, when a conflict between Tshombe and the now 'Lieutenant-General' Mobutu erupted, providing the latter with an opportunity to seize power in a coup, initially 'for five years' – which eventually became 32 years. Tshombe fled back to Spain, but was quick in staging a counter-coup with the support of Belgian interests: a mutiny of some 13,000 Katangese supervised by Belgian officers, broke out in Stanleyville, around the same time with an uprising of pro-Communist fighters led by Gaston Soumialot, better known as the 'Simbas' ('Lions'). The mutineers were joined by the commando regiment of the ANC consisting of the Katangese, now commanded by Colonel Ferdinant Tshipoli. When the Simbas took hostages amongst the white population, Mobutu reacted by deploying the ANC, and Belgian paratroopers launched an airborne operation (*Dragon Rouge)* to recapture Stanleyville and free the majority of hostages.

Undaunted, Tshombe continued trying – until the Hawker Siddeley jet carrying him was hijacked by Francis Bodenan, an agent of the French External Documentation and Counter-Espionage Service (Service de Documentation Extérieure et de Contre-Espionnage, SDECE) while underway from Majorca, and forced to land in Algiers, on 26 June 1967. The Katangan leader was arrested and placed under house arrest: the Algerians resisted all demands for his release and he was never to see the Congo again before dying in 1969.

Nevertheless, on 5 July 1967, another party of mercenaries – including Bob Denard – landed an aircraft at Stanleyville and brought the city under their control, where they were joined by about 3,000 Katangese troops who had mutinied. Mobutu reacted by moving no less than 15,000 ANC troops on Stanleyville: supported not only by Belgian advisors, but also by logistics provided by US advisors, and an air force staffed by CIA-contracted Cuban expatriates; his counteroffensive proved quite effective. An injured Denard was flown out to Salisbury, in Rhodesia, while surviving mercenaries – now led by Belgian Major Jean 'Black Jack' Schramme – retreated, taking numerous hostages with them. While most of the latter were subsequently evacuated by the Red Cross, some were murdered in cold blood, before Schramme withdrew with his force towards his plantation, about 240 kilometres (150 miles) from Stanleyville. After regrouping his troops, he attacked and captured Bukavu on 9 August 1967. Although confronted by a combination of ten-fold stronger ANC units and foreign mercenaries, Schrammes' force managed to hold out for three months before it ran out of ammunition and gave up. The survivors then fled to the neighbouring Rwanda, where they were interned for three months.

As Mobutu's government concentrated its attention upon Bukavu, another mercenary attack into Katanga was launched from Angola on 2 November 1967, this time led by Denard – who had recovered from his earlier injuries. Despite capturing 16 trucks and a train, early on, this intrusion came to nothing. With this, the power of the mercenaries in the Congo was finally destroyed, while Mobutu emerged from these conflicts in relatively firm control over all the major urban and mining areas of the Congo. In turn, his rule drove into exile significant numbers of armed opponents, including not only the surviving leftist insurgents (who continued sporadic actions into eastern Congo), but at least 3,000 of the Katangese, most of whom found refuge in northern Angola. Indeed, as a staunch supporter of Katangan independence and an enemy of Mobutu, the Portuguese colonial authorities were rubbing their hands in

Master of Kleptocracy

Mobutu and his supporters celebrating his take-over in Kinshasa on 16 May 1967. (via Congoforum)

The man who was to play a crucial role in the history of Congo for 37 years was born on 14 October 1930 in Lisali, in what was then the Belgian Congo, of parents from the small Ngbandi ethnic group. In his youth he attended a catholic mission school. Abandoning such a forced education at the time of tough Belgian rules was equal to 'desertion'; however, Mobutu followed his first lover onto the ferry to Leopoldville. Once he was caught, the sentence of seven years in prison was changed to service in the *Force Publique*.

Mobutu, by all accounts, was hungry to learn more about worldwide affairs and was by no means an uneducated artificial African 'corporal dictator'. He read memoires by Churchill and de Gaulle, and Machiavelli's philosophy. Self-taught, he had a column in *Actualites Africaines*, one of only a few Congolese newspapers; but totally under control of the state apparatus of the Belgian Congo. In 1956 he managed to get a job with a more prestigious French language daily printed in Leopoldville, *L'Avenir*. He also befriended the future first prime minister of Congo, Patrice Lumumba. The latter quickly recognized Mobutu's oratory skills and deployed these during the pre-independence negotiations. Once the Congo became independent, Lumumba designated Mobutu the Commander of the ANC. That paid back when the latter was required to tour rioting garrisons and calm down the often-heated atmosphere within the ranks of the military. Mobutu's cordial relations with Lumumba were cut short quite soon afterwards, when he subjected the left-leaning prime minister to a house-arrest at Camp Hardy in Thysville, on 3 December 1960. Recognizing the increasing popularity of the prime minister amongst the troops, and concerned that these might release him, Mobutu and the Belgians organized for Lumumba to be transferred to Katanga. Although visited by Katangese notables – including Tshombe – and Belgian officers over the following days, Lumumba was eventually executed by a firing squad of the Katangan military led by a Belgian mercenary, late in the night of 17 January 1961.

In recognition for this 'success', Mobutu was appointed the Chief-of-Staff ANC by an order of President Kasa-Vubu, officially effective with 23 January 1961. In this position, he was instrumental in crushing the Simba uprising of 1964-1965, which had quickly occupied two thirds of the Congo. When Tshombe and his Congolese National Convention won a large majority in the March 1965 election, but Kasa-Vubu appointed an anti-Tshombe leader, Evariste Kimba, as prime-minister designate, a political crisis erupted which Mobutu exploited to his advantage. Announcing a state of emergency, he assumed sweeping powers and established a highly centralized state in which the parliament was eventually abolished, together with all the political parties. He strictly curtailed the autonomy of the provinces and forced all trade unions to consolidate into a single movement – which was then also brought under government control. Instead, and while wrongly presenting himself as the successor to Lumumba, in 1966 Mobutu instigated the emergence of the Corps of Volunteers of the Republic as a movement designed to mobilize popular support for him. Henceforth, whenever possible, he submitted any kind of opposition through patronage. Whenever impossible, he acted forcefully – through public execution of political rivals, secessionists, true or supposed coup plotters, and anybody else that presented a threat to his rule. In 1966, four cabinet ministers

Continued on page 10

Mobutu meeting U Thant, Secretary General of the UN, in New York in August 1970. (UN photo)

were arrested on charges of complicity in an attempted coup, tried by a military tribunal, and publicly executed in an open-air 'spectacle' witnessed by over 50,000 people. In 1968, Mobutu lured back to Congo one of his arch enemies, Pierre Mulele, Lumumba's Minister of Education and former leader of the Simba Rebellion, with a promise of a national reconciliation and amnesty. As soon as he turned himself in, Mulele was arrested and gruesomely tortured on the personal order from Mobutu: his eyes were gauged out, genitals cut off, and he was still alive when henchmen cut off all of his limbs, one by one. Any armed uprisings were crushed in blood – as was an aborted revolt led by white mercenaries in 1967, usually with help from the USA.

Nevertheless, on the international scene, Mobutu gained notoriety for adjusting his external politics as the wind blew. He maintained close relations with representatives of the CIA, which supported him through direct financing from at least 1962 until the very end of his rule, but also with the PR China and North Korea, in the early 1970s. On the domestic scene, all affairs were under his total control by 1970 – including all elections: for example, in one these his political party won no less than 98.33% of the vote, and in one of his presidential elections Mobutu won 10,131,699 votes with only 157 against him.

In regards of economic affairs, Mobutu became the epitome of 'Kleptocracy': a form of government in which the ruler uses the country and its resources to serve his/her own purposes – and those of the supportive clique. A huge proportion of the income from exports of the Congolese mineral wealth ended in various of his private bank accounts abroad, just as much of the expensive armament and equipment for his military was sold to third parties, and the resulting profit ended up in the pockets of his top civilian and military officers. During a boom of the real estate market in Tokyo, Japan, the local ambassador from the Congo sold the embassy of his country and then had the price transferred to his private bank account.

In 1971, Mobutu embarked on a campaign of pro-Africa cultural awareness, or '*authenticité*'. He not only renamed the country and countless geographic places, and ordered the people of the Congo to drop their European names for African ones, but outright banned Western attire and ties. Three years later, he staged the arguably biggest sport-related media-event ever in the history of Africa. The 'Rumble in the Jungle' as it became widely known, was a heavy-weight boxing-match for the world championship title between George Foreman and Muhammad Ali. For this purpose, Zaire forked out millions of US$ in order to stage the match at a huge stadium outside Kinshasa. Also in 1974, the Zairian football team took part in the World Coup in West Germany – albeit without success.

The period 1975-1978 was probably the most difficult for Mobutu since the mercenary revolt of 1967. Not only that neighbouring Angola came under the control of a 'Marxist' government, but in what he perceived as an insult to his own 'anti-colonialism', his military proved unable to defeat the two insurgent incursions into the Shaba province (formerly Katanga) without help from the French Foreign Legion.

Although remaining in power for another 20 years, Mobutu never recovered from this blow. The principal reason was that he never managed to attract major Western investment again. Nevertheless, his ego continued growing, as did his misuse of state funds for private needs. For many of his foreign trips he would charter a supersonic Aerospatiale-BAC Concorde jet from Air France (which could land at N'Djili International Airport and at Kamina air base, since both had runways longer than 5,000 metres). His corruption, and the corruption of his clique, reached endemic proportions causing such inflation that it led

Continued on page 11

Mobutu with Chinese President Jian Zemin in 1973. (Chinese Internet)

to the cancellation of payments for all debts to foreign creditors. Nevertheless, Mobutu survived again – and then because of his alleged 'anti-communism': Zaire continued receiving substantial aid from the USA and France, and even the International Monetary Fund waived substantial debts thanks to a strong pro-Zaire lobby in major Western capitals.

The situation began to change after the collapse of the Soviet Union in the early 1990s. Meanwhile suffering from an advanced cancer, Mobutu did nothing when the Rwandans launched an invasion of eastern Zaire in 1996, supposedly with the intention of 'repatriating' hundreds of thousands of ethnic Tutsi refugees that fled their homeland during the Rwandan Civil War of 1990-1994. Indeed, the lack of reaction on the part of the Zairian military emboldened the Rwandans to continue their advance west: supported by Uganda and Angola, and reinforced by an alliance of local insurgents, this was approaching Kinshasa by the time Mobutu finally accepted defeat and went into exile, in Morocco, in May 1997. Mobutu died in Rabat on 7 September 1997.

excitement and allowed thousands of the Katangans to settle down.[6]

Kolwezi of 1977-1978

By 1970, the sole remaining threat for Mobutu's rule was that emitted from what was perceived as the Cuban and Soviet-supported government of the Congo-Brazzaville. This was ameliorated, if not resolved, in 1970, by the renewal of diplomatic ties. Firmly in the saddle, Mobutu next decided to lay his hands on the biggest treasure of his country – the mining industry. In 1971, he nationalized all the mining companies in Katanga – including the Belgian-owned Union de Haute-Katanga, incorporated with the Generale Congolaise des Minerals (originally GECOMIN, but renamed into GECAMINES in 1971).[7]

Since Congo became independent, the heart of the country's mining industry became the town of Kolwezi in Katanga, the population of which was estimated at about 143,000. The local mines were operated by the GECAMINES and a few other enterprises: these alone were processing 75% of the copper and 90% of the cobalt ore exported by the country. Without Mobutu's knowledge, though in order to prevent its mines from the catastrophic take-over by the ruling clique from Kinshasa, GECAMINES employed a large number of experts from Europe. Together with their families, these 'expatriates' were concentrated in a settlement directly to the east and west of the main train station, in an area that formed a rectangle of some three by eight kilometres in total: the so-called 'White Rectangle'. There were two airfields nearby: 'Main', with the capacity to take heavy military transports, and the 'Small' one, used by helicopters and light civilian aircraft only.

In contrast to the 'White Rectangle', the districts populated by the Congolese were not far from 'shanty town' status. The majority of the local population came from the Lumba ethnic group, renowned for its opposition to Mobutu's rule. Activists with related ideologies, and also Katangan separatists were strongest in the Manika district of Kolwezi.

In terms of the terrain, the town was surrounded by typical African savannah, the majority of the surface covered by the 2.5m tall "elephant grass", a big obstacle for the observing of enemy positions and movement, and also an easy environment for the

Centrepiece of Western interests in the Congo: one of the copper mines in the Kolwezi area. (Via Daniel Kowalczuk)

Sign at the entrance to the GECAMINES compound in Kolwezi. (Via Daniel Kowalczuk)

FNLC to set up ambushes. South Katanga is a typical African savannah environment, closer in its weather conditions to Angola than to stereotypical "Heart of Darkness" rainforest, associated with Congo. The French and Belgians, when assessing the operations took the presence of the "elephant grass" on board.

Bulwark against Communism

Mobutu's next step was to instigate the change of the country's name to Zaire (actually an early Portuguese transliteration of a Bantu word meaning 'big river'), while renaming himself to Mobutu *Sesse Seko Kuku N'gbendu Wa Za Banga* (the translation of which means 'The all-powerful warrior who, because of his endurance and inflexible will to win, will go from conquest to conquest, leaving fire in his wake'). In similar fashion, all the 'European-sounding' geographic names in Zaire were changed, too: Leopoldville became Kinshasa, Stanleyville was renamed as Kisingani, Elisabethville – the capital of Katanga – was renamed Lubumbashi, while Katanga itself was literally wiped off the maps, and renamed Shaba.

Determined to remain in power at any cost, for the following 20 years Mobutu was foremost busy running an increasingly and pervasively corrupt, despotic regime that mishandled the nation's resources in almost every imaginable fashion – yet enjoyed wholehearted support (and plenty of patience) from major outside powers, primarily the USA and France, as a declared 'bastion of anti-communism'. During the Cold War, the latter often used Congo as a base and a staging ground for supporting various insurgent groups fighting against supposedly pro-Soviet regimes in neighbouring countries, foremost Angola – in return for the provision of financial and military aid to the government.

The majority of insurgents still present in the country followed in fashion: they became preoccupied with the illegal extraction of natural resources, and with smuggling and poaching.

CHAPTER 2
ZAIRIAN MILITARY FORCES

One of the peculiarities of the conflicts fought in southern Zaire of 1977 and 1978 is that it saw the involvement of very diverse military formations, which – generally – could be sorted into no less than six basic categories: the regular armed forces of Zaire, regular and auxiliary insurgents of Zairian origin, Belgian and French armed forces, and various contingents from other armed forces around Africa and the World. While there is not enough space to discuss all the military forces in question, there is at least a need to discuss those of their elements that did become involved, starting with the forces originating from the Congo/Zaire.[8]

Short-Lived Katangan Military

The history of the modern-day armed forces of the Congo – and thus those of Zaire of the mid-1970s – can be traced back to 4 August 1888, when Belgium's King Léopold II, Governor of the Independent State of the Congo, established the *Force Publique*, a private militia composed of foreign mercenaries and Congolese, trained by Belgian officers, and responsible for the protection of economic exploitation. The force was significantly expanded and deployed in combat during the First and Second World Wars, when it became involved in a number of campaigns, mainly in East Africa.

Troops of the *Force Publique* with one of their Belgian officers around the time of the Second World War. (Congoforum)

Upon the independence of the Congo in 1960, the further military build-up then went in two directions. On the side of the government in Kinshasa, and because the *Force Publique* was still run by Belgian officers, there was a mutiny of natives quite soon after independence. The government reacted by rushing to 'Africanize' the ANC's officer corps – although this resulted in massive problems because, after the expulsion of Belgians, the military faced a lack of skills at practically all levels. To remedy the situation, non-commissioned officers (NCOs) above the rank of a sergeant were advanced to officer ranks – but many of these nearly instantly began meddling in politics, resulting in a civil war.

On the contrary, Tshombe depended on European and South African career soldiers to build up an effective and a reliable fighting force: the emerging Katangese military also included a strong air component, equipped with a miscellany of aircraft, including a few Fouga CM.170 Magister training jets. That is how the so-called Katangese National Gendarmerie (*Gendarmerie Nationale Katangaise*) came into being. However, such a designation has never officially existed: it was based on the fact that amongst the people in Francophone former colonies of central Africa any uniformed and armed government force was known as the 'Gendarmerie' and their members as 'Gendarmes'. Indeed, in the former Belgian Congo, even provincial security forces were semi-officially known as 'Gendarmerie'. This is why the short-lived Katangan military of the 1960-1963 period became known as the 'Katangese Gendarmerie' – and is likely to remain known as such.

Schramme's Rebound

When the Katangan secession failed and Tshombe went into exile, in January 1963, it appeared to the UN and Mobutu that the days of the organized Katangan military were numbered. Indeed, the government in Kinshasa even promised to incorporate the Katangese Gendarmerie into the ANC. This was not only easier said than done, but simple wishful thinking. From Mobutu's standpoint, this offer was motivated by the hope that by securing the loyalty of the former commander of the Katangese military – General Norbert Muke – he could motivate Tshombe's supporters into ending any kind of armed resistance. Most of the Katangese recognized this plot: unsurprisingly, despite supervision by UN commissioners, only about a quarter of some 18,000 Katangese troops signed a reconciliation deal – and even fewer were ever integrated into the ANC. The rest – including about 3,500 troops (amongst them Schramme and few of his officers) – fled to Angola, or still roamed around southern Katanga, occasionally also crossing into Northern Rhodesia.[9]

Indeed, when Tshombe was appointed the Prime Minister of the government in Kinshasa, in 1964, he was able to quickly mobilise his ex-soldiers and deploy these to support the ANC's effort to crush the rebellion of the Lumumbists, and then fight the mercenaries in Stanleyville. As mentioned above, at first around 1,600, and then up to 4,500 ex-Katangese troops reinforced the ranks of the ANC in 1964-1965, and helped Tshombe and Mobutu defeat the Simba-uprising. An additional 6,000 were then recruited to form several para-military battalions active in southern Katanga. As of 1966, in addition to about 1,000 mercenaries, about 3,000 former Katangese Gendarmes had fought in South Kivu and the Stanleyville area: it was only the combination of the Tshombe's detention in Algiers and the defeat of the Schramme-led 'mercenary' revolt in Bukavu of June 1967 that forced the survivors to flee to Rwanda and Angola again.

The Good Times

Although an officer training school for the ANC was established in Luluabourg (renamed Kananga in 1971), in early 1961, and this provided relatively good services to the regular Congolese Army, the ANC continued experiencing problems with the reliability of its officers and other ranks. Therefore, as soon as he established himself in power, Mobutu invited six nations to assist in rebuilding the military as an effective fighting force. The result was that Belgium trained the ground forces, Italy the air force, Norway the naval element, Israel the paratroopers and commandos, Canada the communications and transport units, and the USA provided supply and administrative support. With the help of foreign advisers, additional high-level training centres were established by the early 1970s, and these proved so successful that students from other countries – including Burundi, Central African Republic, Chad, Niger, Rwanda and Togo – were trained there as well. However, endemic corruption of the officer corps remained widespread, frequently causing mutinies of different units, irrespectively of the fact that these were all usually staffed by members of the same ethnic group and based in their own territories.

In an attempt to find a solution, Mobutu initiated a major reform of his military in 1968. Under the impression of the effectiveness of the Belgian Army's paratroopers, he extracted all the available 'special' units – like commando and para-commando battalions – to form the Reinforced Airborne Shock-Troops Division, Congo (*Division des Troupes Aéroportées Renforcées de Choc*, DITRAC). Trained by Israeli advisors, the DITRAC was a perfect 'private army': a unit seen as being equally as suitable for protecting Mobutu's rule as for launching high-speed interventions around the country. In practice, it never did anything to justify its 'élite' status, and many of its troops were always 'absent without leave'.

High copper prices of the early 1970s enabled a further military

A company of FAZ troops during a field exercise. (Albert Grandolini Collection)

build-up and Mobutu's government thus continued its reform by placing orders for large amounts of heavy equipment. Eventually at least 220 Panhard AML-60 and AML-90 armoured cars, and 60 Panhard M3 armoured personnel carriers (APCs) were acquire from France to reinforce and replace a miscellany of vintage US-made M3 half-tracks. These enabled the establishment of an armoured car battalion, which was subsequently expanded into an armoured regiment. Furthermore, Zaire acquired up to 525 mortars in calibres from 60 to 120mm, about 80 artillery pieces (including 40 anti-aircraft guns), and 250 recoilless rifles in calibres from 75 to 106mm. FAZ troops were primarily equipped with FN/FAL assault rifles of Belgian origin, FAL light machine guns and MAG medium machine guns. From the USA came such individual weapons as M16 assault rifles, M79 grenade launchers, and LAW anti-tank rockets.

Cooperation with PR China and North Korea

However, these 'good times' were soon over: a dramatic collapse in the prices for copper, endemic corruption and overspending brought Zaire to the brink of a financial meltdown in 1974. After being invited to check the country's balance sheets in the national bank, experts of the International Monetary Fund found out that there was a cash shortfall of about 40% – caused by massive withdrawals by corrupt officials and high-ranking military officers alone. Annoyed by Mobutu's erratic behaviour, the Belgians decided to stay out of this affair: this was little surprising considering that in 1973 Mobutu travelled to the PRC. From that time onwards, Communist China became his new mentors: Mobutu began wearing a 'Mao-style' uniform and demanded that everybody address him as 'Citizen Mobutu'. Before long the FAZ was to benefit from this relationship in the form of orders for 20 Type-63 multiple rocket launchers (MRLs) calibre 107mm, 70 Type-62 light tanks and Type-59 main battle tanks (MBTs), and 12 Type-63 APCs – all of which were delivered between 1974 and 1978. This equipment and Chinese advice were used to establish a mechanised battalion and expand the armoured regiment into the 1st Armoured Brigade. Thus, while the original FAZ was based on a large number of light infantry units, supported by paratroopers and commandos, and specialised for fighting COIN wars, and although climatic circumstances, rugged terrain, dense jungle, lack of roads, and lack of support infrastructure and know-how all but made the operation of large mechanized forces nearly impossible, from the mid-1970s the army became increasingly reliant on armoured formations.[10]

While seeking advice and help in a further military build-up, Mobutu established cooperation with North Korea. So it came to be that the next regular division of the FAZ – the Shaba-based 1st Kamanyola Division – was established in 1974, under the supervision of about 130 North Korean advisors. Eventually, the Zairians proved ill-suited to the harsh North Korean doctrine and training practices: instead of concentrating on proper military training, the latter diverted much of their efforts and time into political indoctrination and the training of political officers. Unsurprisingly, the primary result was additional mutinies – which in turn repeatedly delayed the further training of the Kamanyola Division. Left without a choice, Mobutu was forced to terminate the contract and request that all the North Koreans be withdrawn in 1976, leaving the crucial unit of his military in an only partially-established and partly-trained state.[11]

Further chaos was created by numerous alleged and real coup plots, some of them made up by Mobutu's supporters with the intention of eliminating competition in the FAZ hierarchy. One such plot was quashed in the Kivus (traditionally a 'Lumumbist' region), while others were halted in Badundu, Kasi and Shaba. Each such event resulted in an increase of ethnic rivalries, additional corruption and favouritism, and the waste of resources. Unsurprisingly, the reform of the FAZ from the late 1960s and early 1970s resulted in a failure of gigantic proportions: despite all the spending and the acquisition of immense amounts of armament, ammunition and supplies, and an 'imposing' order of battle, the Zairian military of the mid-1970s was a broken force, entirely unable to defend its homeland. Indeed, as subsequent events were to show, it was unable to run any kind of large-scale operations because it lacked competent officers and the necessary logistical capabilities.

Unsurprisingly, the seven dysfunctional Military Regions (listed in Table 1) were de-facto scrapped: instead, staff officers of Mobutu's military continued using old maps of the *Force Publique*, according to

Table 1: Nominal Structure of the FAZ Ground Forces, 1977-1978

Military Region	HQ	Notes
Direct reporting: DITRAC	Kinshasa	dysfunctional; elements in the process of being reorganized as parts of the 1st Kamanyola Division and other 'elite' units
Direct reporting: 1st Armoured Brigade	Mbanza-Ngungu	Including armoured regiment and mechanized battalion of the future 1st (Independent) Armoured Brigade; still undergoing training
1st Military Region	Kananga	Including two infantry battalions and one support battalion in Kamina
2nd Military Region	Kinshasa	including 311th and 312th Para Battalions and one support battalion; in the process of being expanded into 31st Para Brigade
3rd Military Region	Kisingani	including 411th, 412th, and 413th Commando Battalions and one support battalion
4th Military Region	Lubumbashi	1977: 2nd Airborne Battalion (Lubumbashi), 3rd Commando Battalion (Kamina) 1978: 1st Kamanyola Division (11th, 12th, and 14th Infantry Brigades, each with two infantry battalions and one support battalion) and the 'Leopard' Infantry Battalion
5th Military Region	Bukavu	including Sector Tanganyika with HQ in Kalemie and three infantry battalions
6th Military Region	Mbandaka	
7th Military Region	Goma	

Troops of the 1st Kamanyola Division with their famous uniforms (including the 'Leopard pattern'), and Chinese or North-Korean-made AK-47 variants, during a parade in Kinshasa. (Mark Lepko Collection)

which the country was split into three defence zones – each of which provided the nucleus of one of Kamanyola's brigades. Except for the largely dysfunctional DITRAC and the incomplete Kamanyola, the backbone of the FAZ formed a hodgepodge of 22 shaky infantry battalions (including eight guard battalions), eight commando and para-commando battalions and eight support battalions, with about 35,000 troops (including 1,000 officers and 1,500 NCOs).[12]

Following the visit to Zaire by US Army General James M Rockwell, in 1975-1976, Mobutu decided to expand the FAZ and base at least one 'division' in each of the key provinces. The related military-build up was expected to last 10-12 years, and began through the expansion of existing battalions into brigades. However, this project was far from being realized as of 1977-1978: for example, the French-trained 311th Paratrooper Battalion that was established in late 1977, was about to form the future 31st Paratrooper Brigade. The majority of brigade-sized units were still at only about 30% of their authorised strength.[13]

A FAZ Soldier

There is little doubt that Mobutu wanted the FAZ to become the best-equipped and uniformed army in all of Africa – but also that the results fell well short of his intentions. Apart from such 'flagship' units as the unfortunate Kamanyola Division, most of the rank and file FAZ soldiers were wearing either Belgian type plain uniforms, of the patterns dating from before independence in 1960, or some exported French olive drab uniforms.

Helmets wise, there was large supply of repainted helmets – mainly of US M1 design – left behind by the UN forces on their withdrawal in 1964. As in several other countries of Africa, Zairian soldiers also had the habit of wearing only the plastic inner-helmets, obviously completely useless in combat. Zairean Paras used West German helmets of M71 pattern, the same as Belgian Para Commandoes.

Elite Mobutu formations, like the Paratroopers and Kamanyola members, were better kitted, even if their equipment was anything other than 'standarised'. Even their mid-ranking officers tended to wear a mix of fatigues – like 'duck hunter' camouflage bush hats and French all-arms-type uniforms with 'lizard' camouflage pattern. Indeed, especially in units based away from Kinshasa, it was a common practice for officers to privately buy elements of their

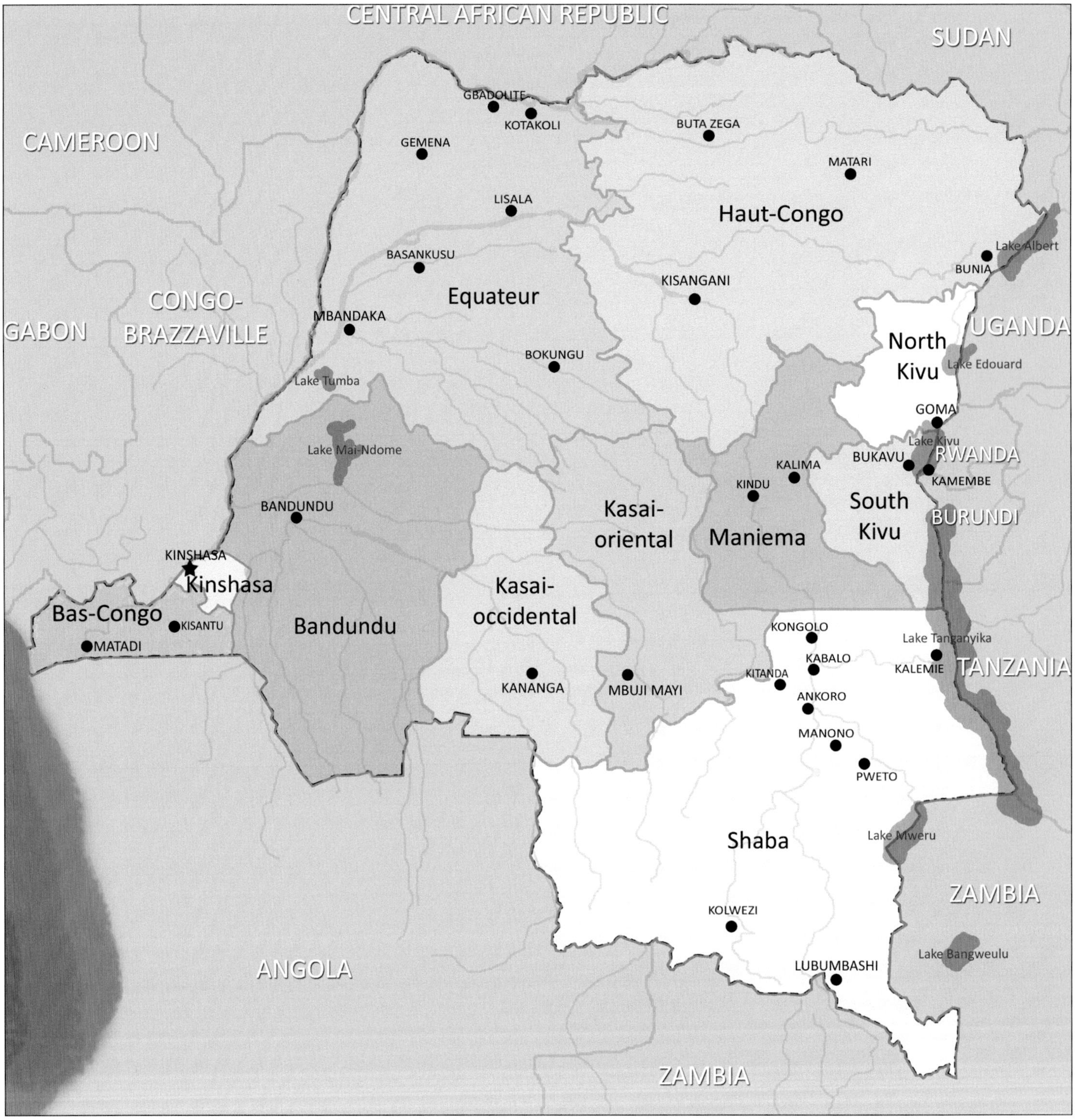

Map of Zaire as organized under Mobutu's rule from 1971. (Map by Tamara Zeller)

uniform. Favoured were diverse camouflage-patterned blouses and trousers, and garments that signalled 'prestige'.

Zairian paras were issued with uniforms of non-specified origin, thought to be privately-made in Belgium. These included a pattern with close resemblance to Mobutu's favourite carnivore – the leopard – and these were proudly displayed on parade and widely worn by units that were deployed during the two Shaba wars. However, the supply chain for them was soon exhausted: as the stock of 'leopard' camouflaged uniforms dried up, several of its elements were mixed with all other available bits and pieces, creating a rather bizarre, 'guerrilla-style' appearance for many of FAZ's battalions. Mobutu's crack units used mainly Chinese made versions of the omni-present AK-47 assault rifle, with the addition of some FN-FAL assault rifles and in second line units a few SAFN 49 rifles, mixed with even older French MAS 36 rifles.[14]

Force Aérienne Zaïroise

Considering local terrain and climate, and the poor land communications, but also that almost 100 airfields and airstrips, as well as four major air bases were left behind by the Belgians, it is unsurprising that air power played an important role in the capabilities of the Zairian military, and that it experienced a phase of significant development during the 1960s and 1970s.

Established on independence as the '*Aviation de la Force Republique du Congo*', the Zairian Air Force (*Force Aérienne Zaïroise*, FAZA) as it was in the mid-1970s, came into being during the second half of the

A group of troops from the 1st Kamanyola Division manning a checkpoint during the II Shaba War, in 1978. Note that the – by then 'usual' – mix of Leopard pattern uniforms and diverse other fatigues. (Albert Grandolini Collection)

A group of FAZ troops as seen in the southern Shaba province In May 1978, wearing a mix of uniforms, caps and fatigues quite representative for that period. Note that their armament consisting of FN/FAL and M16 assault rifles. (Albert Grandolini Collection)

leader of their team was severely injured. Overall, by early 1963, only 11 Congolese pilots, 38 technicians and two aerial-photo-interpreters had completed their training with Italian help, but none of them was considered combat-capable and thus they saw no action during the civil war that was to rage until 1967. Nevertheless, the Italians remained influential and launched a new effort, advising the government in Kinshasa to purchase 15 Piaggio P.148 basic trainers, which proved more suitable for initial pilot training. A training squadron equipped with that type was established in October 1964, by which time the balance of the air force consisted of the US-run Anstalt Wigmo contingent manned by exiled Cuban pilots that flew a miscellany of North American T-28 Trojans, Douglas B-26K Invaders, Curtiss C-46 Commando and Beechcraft C-45 transports, as well as Bell 47 and Vertol-Piasecki H-21 helicopters.[15]

The following year, one group of Congolese pilots was sent to Marignane in France, to be trained on Aérospatiale SE.316B Alouette III helicopters, 15 of which were purchased, while a few pilots were converted to 12 additional T-6s, purchased from France. At least four of these aircraft were lost in fighting against mercenaries in May 1967,

1960s. A very few native pilots and ground personnel were trained by Belgian instructors (and one former Luftwaffe Colonel) on a small number of North American T-6G Texans in the early 1960s, before Italy was contracted to take over the role of major supervisor for the fledgling air force.

The Italians established a pilot training school at N'Dolo airfield, in 1962, equipped with some ten T-6s provided from surplus stocks of their air force, but this was closed shortly afterwards following a series of fatal and near-fatal accidents, including one in which the

when six of the Congolese pilots flew their first combat sorties on T-28s.[16]

Meanwhile, the air force was reorganized into two groups, each of which had three wings, in turn consisting of three squadrons, in November 1966. The No.1 Group included the 11th Transport Wing, mainly manned by foreigners that flew transport aircraft, and the 12th Tactical Support Wing, equipped with T-6s and Alouettes, and manned by Congolese and Belgian crews. The Italian-run training squadron was expanded to become the 13th

An AML-90 armoured car (foreground) and an AML-60 (background) of the FAZ. Note that the 'registration plate' – applied directly on the front hull: this included two strips in national colours (with inscription 'FAZ' in green on the yellow field), and the hull-number applied in white. (Albert Grandolini Collection)

One of the multiple new types to enter service in Congo/Zaire of the late 1960s and early 1970s was the Aerospatiale SE.316B Alouette III, 15 of which were acquired starting in 1965. This photograph of the example with serial '359' was taken in 1966. (Pit Weinert Collection)

Two SF.260MC trainers as seen at Kamina Air Base, shortly after their delivery in 1971. (Aermacchi)

Wing, consisting of one preparatory pilot training squadron (responsible for recruitment and selection), one elementary pilot training squadron, and one advanced training squadron. However, the No.2 Group still consisted exclusively of Anstalt Wingmo crews and their US-supplied aircraft and helicopters, most of which were withdrawn from Congo by 1968 and re-deployed to South-East Asia. In order to re-equip the No.2 Group, in April of the same year, the Congolese and Italians signed a new treaty regarding technical assistance, and in May 1968, the air force launched a big recruitment campaign, intending to find and train enough new pilots to replace the foreigners. Simultaneously, a decision was taken to purchase 17 Aermacchi MB.326 jet-trainers (nick-named Sukisa by the

The first of seven C-130Hs acquired by the FAZA received the registration 9T-TCA. The fleet saw intensive service during the 1970s in particular. (Martin Hornliman/Milpix Collection)

The sixth Zairian C-130H (construction number 4588) was originally registered as 9T-TCF. Like the rest of the fleet, it took part in the I and II Shaba Wars, before being impounded in Italy, in 1982, and later sold back to France. (Tom Cooper Collection)

One of three DHC-5D Buffalos purchase by Zaire in the early 1970s. Externally, they closely resembled C-7As operated by the USAF during the Vietnam War. (Albert Grandolini Collection)

Congolese) and 12 SIAI-Marchetti SF.260MC piston-engined trainers, and corresponding contracts were signed soon after.[17]

Furthermore, in relation to the establishment of the DITRAC, Mobutu convinced the administration of the US president Richard Nixon to grant permission for delivery of seven Lockheed C-130H Hercules transports and three de Havilland Canada DHC-5D Buffalo transports in June 1971. Around the same time, the fleet of light transports, liaison and training aircraft was further reinforced through the acquisition of 16 Reims-Cessna FRA.150M and FTB.337Gs (which could be armed and used as light fighter-bombers), and the helicopter fleet through 5 additional Alouette IIIs.[18]

Table 2: Zairian MB.326GBs, 1969-1978			
Serial Number	Construction Number	Delivery Date	Notes
FG-460	6460	1969	last seen in 1993
FG-461	6461	1969	last seen in 1981
FG-462	6462	1969	
FG-463	6463	1970	
FG-464	6464	1970	
FG-465	6465	1970	
FG-466	6466	1970	ex I-MANA
FG-467	6467	1970	ex I-MANO, last seen 1981
FG-468	6468	1970	ex I-MANP, destroyed in May 1978
FG-469	6469	1970	ex I-MANQ, last seen May 1978
FG-470	6470	1970	ex I-MANR, last seen 1975
FG-471	6471	1970	ex I-MANS, written off in May 1978
FG-472	6472	1970	ex I-MANY, last seen 1978
FG-473	6473	1970	ex I-MAOA, written off in May 1978
FG-474	6474	1970	ex I-MAOB, last seen 1980
FG-475	6475	1970	ex I-MAOC
FG-476	6476	1970	ex I-MANX, accident at Kolwezi, 1977, last seen 1980

The Way Forward: the Aermacchi MB.326 Sukisa Deal

During the 1960s, Mobutu signed numerous large contracts with diverse Italian businesses. Therefore, few were surprised when on 16 April 1968, his Chief of Staff FAZ, General Louis de Gonzac Bobozo, announced to the Chief of the Italian Air Force's Mission to Zaire, General Antonio Pappalardo, their intention to obtain jet trainers with secondary combat capability from Italy, with the aim of replacing remaining T-28s and B-26s. Related negotiations resulted in an order with Aermacchi at Varese for 17 MB.326GB jet trainers and close support aircraft, signed later the same year. This order was followed by another, for 12 SIAI-Marchetti SF.260MC piston-engined trainers, and a contract for the provision of technical assistance by Italian advisors. Simultaneously, the air force launched a major recruitment campaign, intending to find and train enough new pilots to replace all the foreigners that still served within its ranks as of that time.[19]

For reasons of prestige, Mobutu demanded the delivery of the first batch of MB.326GBs on time for a military parade that was to be held in Kinshasa on 24 November 1969. Correspondingly, three Congolese pilots – including Lieutenant Azanga – underwent a conversion course for the type at Aermacchi's facility in Lecce, Italy, while the first three jets (serials FG-460, FG-461, and FG-462) reached N'Djili IAP, following a lengthy delivery flight over all of northern and central Africa, just a day before the parade. In Zairian service, the type received the nick-name 'Sukisa'[20]

As additional Zairian pilots were converted to the type, the Sukisas were declared operational with the 11th Squadron FAZA, based on the military side of the giant N'Djili International Airport (IAP), south-east of Kinshasa, in early 1970. In June of the same year, they were involved in the first big exercise of the FAZ and the FAZA, staged to demonstrate the new capabilities and skills of the growing force. Thus, as of 1972 the FAZA – headquartered at Ndolo airport, south-west of Kinshasa – was re-organized into three commands:

- Central Operational Command;
- Air Force School Command, and
- Technical and Logistics Command.

Equipped with a miscellany of about 60 diverse aircraft and helicopters left behind from earlier times, it was still a diminutive force of about 760 personnel, including 55 pilots, 16 flight engineers, 10 radio operators, and 81 pilot-trainees. Only 5 out of 36 of the originally delivered North American T-28 remained, providing advanced training and a limited strike capability, but these were meanwhile in the process of being replaced by SF.260MCs and MB.326s. The transport component included a collection of 15 Douglas C-47, Douglas C-54, Fairchild C-118s and Lockheed C-130Hs of US-origin, while the single helicopter squadron operated a mix of nine SNCA Sud-Est (later Aerospatiale) SE.3150/318C Alouette II and SE.3160/316B Alouette III, and Aerospatiale SA.330C Puma helicopters, organized as listed in Table 3. As well a large Italian team, the FAZA was supported by French technicians contracted via a dedicated private company, the SODEMAZ – created by Lockheed (nowadays Lockheed-Martin): this provided most of the maintenance for the transports and helicopters. However, the air force was plagued by exactly the same problems as FAZ's ground force: standards of conduct and behaviour were miserable, standards of maintenance minimal, officers were heavily corrupt, and regularly sold kerosene and spare parts on the black market, while the pool of native ground personnel (especially technical specialists) was nearly non-existent. For example, as of August 1975 only two C-130s, one DC-4 and two C-47s were operational, and only 15 out of the original MB.326s were still intact. Part of the reason for this situation was the rapid expansion: the government continued placing orders for additional aircraft and helicopters, while under-estimating the need to recruit and train enough native personnel for these.[21]

Despite continuous Italian supervision, and the presence of a technical team from Aermacchi, the efforts to train Congolese pilots and ground crews were only partially successful. Between 1969 and through the early 1970s, the Italian-run training unit – meanwhile expanded into the 13th Wing – received an average intake of around 40 native students a year, but less than half of these had completed

Table 3: FAZA Flying Units, 1977-1978			
Unit	Base	Type	Notes
1st Air Group (HQ Kinshasa)			
12th Liaison Wing			
112th Squadron 122nd Squadron	N'Dolo N'Dolo	SA.316B, Bell 47G SA.330C	
13th Training Wing			(13e EdE)
131th Elementary Training Squadron	N'Dolo	FRA.150, SF.260MC	
132nd Advanced Training Squadron	N'Djili	MB.326GB	
19th Transport Wing			(19e EdAL)
191ere Escadrille	N'Djili	C-130H	
2nd Air Group (HQ Kamina)			
21st Attack and Assault Wing			(21er EdCA)
211th Squadron	Kamina	Mirage 5M, Mirage 5DM	
212th Squadron	Kamina	MB.326GB	
22th Tactical Transport Wing			(22e EdTT)
221th Squadron	Kamina	DHC-5D, Cessna 310R	

their training. Out of 720 candidates applying to become pilots in 1971, only 20 were accepted, and only 13 sent to Italy for advanced training on MB.326s: the other seven were sent to France instead, where they were trained as helicopter pilots. Reasons were diverse and ranged from problems with students, numerous fatal accidents and foreigners not being interested in providing the best service simply because their employers were not interested in losing their lucrative contracts. Thus, the number of fully-qualified pilots and ground crews increased only gradually during the mid-1970s, enabling the FAZA to reorganize the fleet into two units: the 120th Squadron and the 132nd Squadron, both of which were originally a part of the 13th Wing, and based at N'Djili and Ndolo.[22]

All of the 17 MB.326GBs were delivered by 1975, when the Italians declared the FAZA as 'self-sufficient in operations and maintenance' of the MB.326 and SF.260, and withdrew their military mission from Zaire. Around the same time, the Sukisa-fleet was reorganized once again: the 132nd Squadron remained with the 13th Wing at N'Djili, while the rest of the fleet was formed into the 212th Squadron and re-deployed to Kamina AB, in Shaba, where it became a part of the newly-established 21st Wing. Moreover, the fleet continued suffering from poor reliability: the pilots selected to fly Sukisas, for instance, were promoted to their positions due

The first group of Congolese/Zairian pilots to undergo conversion training for MB.326s at Lecce, in Italy. (Pit Weinert Collection)

Right-hand view of the MB.326GB serial FG-460 – the first of the Sukisas destined for Zaire. Note that the early-style of the canopy, with a single-piece transparent hood. (Pit Weinert Collection)

Left-hand view of the same MB.326GB. Notable are wing-tip mounted drop-tanks: the out-sides of these were painted in day-glo orange, in-sides in matt black. Also of interest is the underwing drop tank, painted in same colours as used in the camouflage pattern on the fuselage. (Pit Weinert Collection)

Top view of the MB.326GB Sukisa serial FG-460, revealing details of the camouflage pattern and original – 'Congolese' – national markings: these were replaced by insignia of the FAZA, applied starting in late 1971. (Pit Weinert Collection)

to their political and tribal connections, rather than flying skills.[23] In similar fashion, the fleets of C-130H Hercules and DHC-5 Buffalo transports were re-organized and re-distributed as listed in Table 3.

Star of the Show: Mirage

Having successfully concluded the acquisition of MB.326s, in 1972 Zairian officials began approaching French representatives in Kinshasa with enquiries regarding a possible purchase of Dassault Mirage 5 supersonic fighter-bombers. Resulting negotiations were protracted, not only because the manufacturer was overwhelmed with orders from about a dozen other export customers, but especially because there were serious doubts that the

A pre-delivery photograph of the MB.326GB serial FG-469. For its transfer flight to Zaire, the aircraft received a civilian registration (and call-sign), I-MANQ. FG-469 is known to have flown combat sorties during the I Shaba War, in 1977. (Pit Weinert Collection)

Probably taken following its overhauls – perhaps even after repairs necessary due to the damage it suffered during the II Shaba War – this photograph shows the third Zairian Sukisa: the MB.326GB FG-463, in full FAZA markings, but in Italy, in the early 1980s. (Tom Cooper Collection)

FAZA could operate as advanced and complex a combat aircraft. Nevertheless, a combination of Zairian pressure and 'higher interests of national security' eventually resulted in Paris giving in: in late 1973, Kinshasa placed an order for 14 Mirage M5M fighter-bombers and interceptors and 3 Mirage 5DM two-seat conversion trainers.

The conversion of FAZA pilots and technicians to Mirages was undertaken in Dijon, France. Pierre Grosjean, then a pilot-instructor with the AdA's training unit Escadre de Chasse d'Entrainament (ECT) 2/2, 'Côte d'Or', recalled:

> I had three Zairian trainees on the Mirage IIIBE: Lieutenant Leon M'Bo (six flights between 12 September 1974 and 8 October 1975), Lieutenant Guillaume Bafuma Limpaka (on 26 February 1976), and Lieutenant Kabeya, on 16 April 1976.[24]

Conversion training of Zairian pilots continued in Dijon from July 1977, on two FAZA Mirage 5DMs and one Mirage 5M, and until the students completed their training with Fighter Squadron (*Escadre de Chasse*, EC) 3/3, 'Ardennes', at Nancy-Ochey AB.

Because Dassault was overburdened with orders from a range of overseas customers, there was a delay in delivery of the first three Zairian Mirages. With the original contract stipulating the first delivery in time for Mobutu's 10th anniversary of seizure of power, in 1975, France was forced to loan Zaire three Mirage 5Fs for the festivities in Kinshasa. The related operation was launched on 13 October 1975, and saw the transfer of the first Zairian 5DMs (serials M201 and M202) and three Mirage 5Fs of EC 3/13 'Auvergne' from Colmar in north-eastern France, to Zaire. For this flight, the Mirage 5Fs wore makeshift Zairian markings, and were modified through the addition of VHF-radios, compatible with those used for air traffic control in Africa. Supported by two C.160 Transall transports of the AdA, the aircraft barely made it to Kinshasa on time. Furthermore, while permitting the return of two Transalls, Mobutu blocked the return of three loaned Mirage 5Fs, conditioning their release on deliveries of Mirage 5Ms.

The second delivery took place on 18 March 1976, when 5Ms with serials M401, M402, M403, and M404 – accompanied by two C.160s of the AdA – were transferred from Bordeaux-Mérignac via Rabat (Morocco), Las Palmas (Canary Islands, Spain), Dakar (Senegal), Bamako (Mali), Abidjan (Ivory Coast), Lomé (Togo), Liberville (Gabon) to N'Djili, in the course of a two-days long odyssey. One of involved pilots, Pierre-Alain Antoine (he flew the M402) recalled:

> We had to hold off our arrival over the runway at Kinshasa so that

Lieutenant Mukendi Kabanga, a Zairian student-pilot seen together with a Mirage IIIB of the ECT 2/2, in Dijon in 1976. Kabanga went on to become a commercial pilot, flying Boeing 737s for Air Zaire and then its replacement, Lignes Aériennes Congolaises. (Arnaud Delallande Collection)

Captain M'Bo could join us for an overflight of the city and a flypast over Mobutu's palace. Unfortunately, M'Bo had a tyre burst during taxiing out in a Mirage so he joined our four Mirages in a Beechcraft for the flight over the palace's balcony.

It was only a week later that the three borrowed Mirage 5Fs were granted permission to return to France.

The final delivery flight included no less than eight aircraft, 14 pilots and 37 mechanics. Run as Operation *Koba*, it took place on 27 November 1976. With this, the *211e Escadrille*, an element of the *21er Escadre de Chasse et d'Assaut* (21st Fighter/Assault Squadron), part of the *2 Groupement Aérien* (2nd Air Group), based at Kamina AB, in Shaba, was nearly complete: due to financial problems, the last three single seaters were never delivered to Zaire. The 21st Squadron thus only received eight 5Ms and three 5DMs – and no less than two of the two-seaters had been written-off in accidents already by 1978.[25]

Other than its deployment in Chad as a

The 'first Mirage made for Zaire': two-seater Mirage M5DM, serial 'M201', as seen prior to delivery. (Tom Cooper Collection)

For their transfer-flight to Zaire, FAZA's Mirages usually received big French national markings (and some unit insignia) applied on the fin – but still wore their genuine serials. This photograph of the Mirage M5DM 'M202' was taken at Liberville, in Gabon, on 30 March 1976, while the jet was crewed by the French pilot Pierre-Alain Antoine. (Photo by M. Fluet-Lecerf, via Pit Weinert)

Background of Mirage 5M

In 1966, Israel contracted Dassault Aviation to develop the Mirage V (later re-designated Mirage 5), as a ground-attack variant of the Mirage IIIE. Intending to purchase a licence to manufacture the new variant at the newly-established Aircraft Project Administration of Israel (which subsequently evolved into the Israel Aircraft Industries, IAI), the Israelis also sent a group of engineers to France.

The related research and development work proceeded quite quickly: the Mirage V retained the classic platform of its predecessor, but received a slightly stretched fuselage. Like the Mirage IIIE, the cockpit was moved slightly forward in comparison to the original Mirage IIIC. The avionics complex of the Mirage IIIE was greatly simplified and installed in a slightly longer, yet slender nose. In turn, the extra space behind the cockpit was used to install additional fuel cells. The first prototype of the new variant flew for the first time on 19 May 1967. However, only two weeks later, on 2 June 1967, Paris imposed its first arms embargo upon Israel and further cooperation was officially cancelled.

Supposedly as a result of this decision, Israel never received the 30 Mirage 5Js, 50% of which were paid up-front, and which were already in the process of manufacture, nor the 20 additional examples that were originally ordered as an 'option'. The situation should, in theory, then have worsened after French President Charles de Gaulle imposed the second, 'total' arms embargo on Israel, in January 1969, in reaction to repeated Israeli attacks on Lebanon.

Actually, both of the embargos were only partial, and nearly everything publicly announced about this affair was just part of a cover-up: not only was Israel permitted to continue purchasing spare parts for aircraft delivered before the June 1967 War, but cooperation between Israel and Dassault subsequently continued in a discreet fashion. Indeed, Israel continued transferring payments for the total of 50 Mirage 5Js that were meanwhile on order even after Paris and Tel Aviv publicly entered negotiations about the return of the payments in question, officially concluded only in February 1972. Meanwhile, the AdA officially agreed to buy 50 Mirage 5Js built for the IDF/AF but impounded in France.

Instead, and as early as of January 1968, Dassault signed a new contract with a consortium created by the IAI and Rockwell International, of the USA, for a delivery of 50 Mirage 5s to Israel in the form of knockdown assembly kits. In order to further increase the cover-up, Dassault ordered various subassemblies for these aircraft to be manufactured by a wide variety of sub-contractors, including Aerospatiale. The Reims-Cessna company manufactured wings and fuselages, while Dassault manufactured only the front fuselages for 10 two-seaters that were delivered extra, as a part of a follow-up order, in the early 1970s. Delivered to Israel on board US transport aircraft, the Mirages were then assembled with the help of well-versed engineers provided by Rockwell. This is how IAI actually came into being. Israel thus very much received its 50 Mirage 5Js from France, even though these were subsequently declared as 'IAI Nesher' (or 'Dagger', when re-exported to Argentina).

Due to the success of Israeli-operated Mirages in combat in the Middle East, Dassault was meanwhile overwhelmed with additional orders from elsewhere: representatives of about a dozen different countries queued up for Mirage 5s – although this variant turned out to be slightly heavier, less manoeuvrable and slower in acceleration than the earlier Mirage IIIC. On the African continent, South Africa, Gabon and Libya placed large orders, followed by Saudi Arabia – which placed a huge order on behalf of Egypt: at nearly the same point in time, the French were thus almost simultaneously delivering fighter bombers to Israel and its most bitter enemies. Unsurprisingly considering its military links to Israel, Zaire followed in fashion.[26]

part of an African peace-keeping mission, the Zairian Mirage-fleet saw very little further operational service. By 1988, only seven 5Ms and one 5DMs remained intact. The government in Kinshasa then sold them back to Dassault, which used the aircraft as sources of spares while overhauling Egyptian Mirage 5s. Only one Zairian Mirage M5M survived intact: declared irreparable following an emergency landing at N'Djamena IAP in 1983, the M403 was evacuated to Zaire in 1990, and subsequently sold to the owner of a small, ultralight airfield in central France. It remains on display there until today.

Table 4: FAZA Mirage 5s, 1975-1988

Variant	Serial	Fate
Mirage 5M	M401	Written off 8 December 1978
Mirage 5M	M402	Damaged at N'Djamena IAP, 1983; sold to France in 1990
Mirage 5M	M403	
Mirage 5M	M404	
Mirage 5M	M405	
Mirage 5M	M406	
Mirage 5M	M407	
Mirage 5M	M408	
Mirage 5M	M409	not delivered; sold to Venezuela as Mirage 50 instead
Mirage 5M	M410	not delivered; sold to Venezuela as Mirage 50 instead
Mirage 5M	M411	not delivered; sold to Gabon instead
Mirage 5M	M412	not delivered; sold to Venezuela as Mirage 50 instead
Mirage 5M	M413	not delivered; sold to Egypt as Mirage 5SDDE '9161' instead
Mirage 5M	M414	not delivered; sold to Gabon instead
Mirage 5DM	M201	written off by 1978
Mirage 5DM	M202	written off 8 December 1978
Mirage 5DM	M203	

CHAPTER 3
FOREIGN MILITARY FORCES

As of the mid-1970s, the French armed forces were still undergoing wide-ranging reforms initiated by former President Charles de Gaulle in the 1960s, and thus represented a mix of old and new ideas. Totalling about 324,000 officers and other ranks (including its own aviation), the French Army was predominantly a conscript force, and accounted for about 65.7% of the total military strength. Its primary units were four armoured divisions, two infantry divisions, and one each of alpine, airborne, and paratrooper divisions. Furthermore, there existed seven armoured car regiments and two motorized infantry regiments. With the defence spending being limited to the moderate 4.67% of the annual national budget, many of troops were still equipped with equipment left over from the wars in Indochina and Algeria, while modern systems – whether with regards to small arms, or in the case of guided missiles – remained relatively scarce. The mass of units and equipment were deployed for the purpose of facing a possible Soviet-led Warsaw Pact invasion of France or in Western Germany.

In comparison, French forces still deployed in Africa were diminutive in size – even if imposing a heavy strain upon the logistic chain of the entire military. Their majority were deployed in a sort of corridor across the continent, roughly along the spine of the former French Equatorial Africa: about 1,000 were in Senegal, 450 in Gabon, and 400 in Ivory Coast; by far the biggest contingent (about 1,500 troops) were present in Chad, where it maintained an air base with depot. Their primary objective was the support of, and training for, friendly governments and military forces, several of which were facing the threat of Communist-backed insurgencies. Furthermore, France also maintained diverse detachments in all of her overseas territories, including French Polynesia, New Caledonia, French Guyana, Martinique, Guadeloupe and Saint Pierre et Miquelon.

Paratroopers of the Foreign Legion

Since its foundation in 1831 the Foreign Legion has been dogged with controversy. Its main purpose was always the same: to fight colonial wars on behalf of French interests. Ever since that date the Legion was present on all fronts of virtually every war France was involved in. First in Algeria, then Crimea, Italy, Mexico, Tonkin,

Paratroopers of the 2e REP as seen while preparing for a training jump. (Foreign Legion release, via Daniel Kowalczuk)

Paratroopers of the 2e REP as seen on their arrival at N'Djili IAP, in Zaire, on the morning of 19 May 1978. All were wearing the 'Satin 300' combat uniform, with some of their own adaptations, and the French ranger boots. (Albert Grandolini Collection)

Table 5: Organization of the 2e REP, May 1978		
Unit	Role	Notes
1st Company	command & anti-tank	CO: Colonel Erulin Chief-of-Staff: Lieutenant-Colonel Benezit Operations Officer: Captain Coevoet Intelligence Officer: Captain Thomas Signals Officer: Adjutant-Chief Kohler Air Force Liaison Officer: Commander Amice Support Officer: Captain Quiniou Chief of the Support Element: Lieutenant Jambu Technical Officer: Adjutant-Chief Achenbrenner Commander of Protection Element: Lieutenant Leroux Chief Doctor: Medical-Commander Ferret Assistant Doctor: Medical-Captain Morcillo Quartermaster: Sergeant Lallemand
Support Element	support	CO Captain Legrand Deputy CO: Captain Halbert Commander Mortar Section 81: Lieutenant Verna
1st Company	combat	CO Captain Poulet Deputy CO: Captain de Richoufftz Chief of the Command Section: Warrant Officer Hosteins Chief of Combat Section: Lieutenant Rochon Leader of Combat Section: Lieutenant Puga Adjutant to the Chief of Combat Section: Adjutant-Chief Pou
2nd Company	combat	CO: Captain Dubos Deputy CO: Lieutenant Good Adjutant to the Chief of the Command Section: Adjutant-Chief Schyns Chief of Combat Section: Lieutenant Raymond (wounded on 20 May 1978) Chief of Combat Section: Sergeant-Chief Milesie Chief of Combat Section: Sergeant-Chief Aoustet
3rd Company	combat	CO: Captain Gaussers Deputy CO: Lieutenant Banal Adjutant to the Chief of the Command Section: Adjutant-Chief Hessler Chief of Combat Section: Lieutenant Bourgain Chief of Combat Section: Lieutenant Wilhem Chief of Combat Section: Warrant-Officer Ivanov
4th Company	combat	CO: Captain Grail Deputy CO: Captain Jolivet Adjutant to the Chief of the Command Section: Warrant-Officer Dapont Chief of Combat Section: Lieutenant Dary Chief of Combat Section: Lieutenant Philipponnat Chief of Combat Section: Sergeant-Chief Case
Reinforcements		Lieutenant Lavergne (Team Leader for Communications) Lieutenant Prut (Team Leader for Communications)
Detachment of Military Air Transport		CO Detachment of C.160: Lieutenant-Colonel Bernier Commander Roy (liaison officer) Captain Teikido (pilot) Captain Florysiak (pilot) Captain Simon (liaison officer) Captain Heliard (liaison officer) Lieutenant Fromageot (pilot) Lieutenant Henry (liaison officer) Chief Warrant Officer Mengele

While taken at the end of the Foreign Legion's deployment to Zaire, this photograph is notable for showing the primary means of identification for Legion's paras during that operation: a scarf in company's colours wrapped around the left shoulder. (Albert Grandolini Collection)

Dahomey, France itself, Madagascar, the First World War, Morocco, Syria, the Second World War (during which its various units declared loyalty to both sides – Vichy and Free France), Indochina (with an approximate strength of 35,000 soldiers, the highest ever), the Suez War of 1956, back to Algeria and finally Kolwezi. The significance of Kolwezi is that the Foreign Legion was desperately seeking the justification of its existence – following a disastrous involvement in the mutiny of the French military and subsequent disbandment of the 1e REP. The intervention in Zaire thus provided the perfect chance to redeem their reputation. It is fair to say that despite many obstacles, improvisation on a large scale and lack of coordination with the Belgians, 2e REP gave good account overall, with a professional approach to the task.

Indeed, what was to become the main strike force of the French military in Zaire in 1978 was the 2e REP. Originally established as a battalion in Morocco, in 1948, a year later this unit was re-deployed to Indochina, where it took part in the famous Battle of Dien Bien Phu in 1954, during which it lost a total of 775 soldiers. Next on its list of battle honours was Algeria: during the war there, the unit was expanded into a regiment, and took place in every major action until its withdrawal in 1961.

Six years later, all the elements of the Foreign Legion were incorporated into the regular French Army. Correspondingly, the 2e REP became a part of the 2nd Para Brigade, itself an element of the 11th Airborne Division. The unit saw relatively little action during the following years, with the exception of running a security operation in Djibouti when that country was granted independence in 1977.

At the time, the 2e REP consisted of four companies with specialized tasks, and a mortar platoon, as listed in Table 5, and was commanded by Colonel Phillipe Erulin. Its overall strength was about 700 – roughly comparable to a battalion of the US Army's rangers.

Paratroopers of the 2e REP were dressed in the regular "Satin 300" combat uniform (*tenue de combat Mle 1963*), although with some Foreign Legion adaptations. That included a tailored shorter jacket, and narrow trousers. Many Legionnaires, specifically more experienced ones and NCOs also had bayonets attached to their webbing. Multi-pocketed grenade bags were very popular, along with pouches to stash cleaning accessories for personal weapons. The French version of ranger boots were worn (based on the US WWII-model). Headgear consisted of the famous Foreign Legion green beret with the 2e REP variant of French Paras' standard badge. NCOs and officers usually had their rank chevrons fixed onto the material with a Velcro patch. In Kolwezi the recognition sign for troops were scarfs, worn whenever possible over the left shoulder. Companies as follows: *1er*- green; *2e* – red; *3e* – black; *4e* – light grey; *CCS* (Combat and Services Company) – yellow and CEA (Reconnaissance and Support Company) – blue.

In terms of the webbing equipment, 2e REP in Kolwezi used a US based design with French modifications. That included pouches for MAT-49 magazines, the above-mentioned weapon-cleaning kit pouch, water bottle attachment buckle and secondary weapon ammunition pouch (pistols and sometimes sniper rifle rounds). There was also a small first aid pouch, attached to the shoulder strap. Many soldiers, however, carried much bigger "commando style" first aid packs, these consisted of dressings, gas antidote, morphine, salt pills, halazone and dexadrine and an ointment for combat-sustained burns.

Helmets used for the Kolwezi jumps, were the Mle 1956 paratroopers' version of the standard French Mle 1951 helmet.

Paras jumping into Kolwezi had very little equipment for the initial stage of the operation. "Must-have" items included a special poncho rolled under the rucksack, very often a green zipped cardigan (helpful to deal with the savannah's cold nights) and in some cases additional food rations and canteen.

Each platoon was also issued with a number of coloured identification triangles to be worn on the back of each soldier.

Small arms included the MAT-49 submachine gun, FR F1 sniper rifle and MAC 50 pistol. One interesting story relates to the fact that there are numerous photos showing Legionnaires carrying G3 assault rifles of German origin. These were, in-fact, captured in Kolwezi and picked-up by individual soldiers for temporary use, due to its efficiency. The unorthodox Foreign Legion cadre did not mind that fact, as long as at the end of the operation quartermasters could account for the exact number of weapons and types as taken from the regimental arsenal when leaving 2e REP HQ in Corsica.

Belgian Armed Forces

Since the independence of the Congo, in 1960, followed by the independence of Rwanda and Burundi in 1962, Belgium lost all of her overseas territories, and its military saw no commitments abroad and was therefore greatly downsized. Nevertheless, because Belgium was also a member of NATO, it was obliged to contribute to the collective defence. Correspondingly, out of about 63,400 officers and other ranks that served in the mid-1970s, a force of up to 27,000 was regularly rotated into West Germany, and the military maintained a trained reserve of about 50,000 (with an intake of about 10,000 new recruits every year). While not as complex as the French, the order of battle of the Belgian armed forces, most of which was committed to its NATO role, included one armoured and three mechanised infantry brigades; three reconnaissance battalions; two motorized infantry battalions; one parachute-commando regiment; three artillery battalions; one battalion of surface-to-surface missiles and two of surface-to-air missiles; five engineer battalions, and four squadrons of army aviation.

For the Belgian intervention in Zaire of 1978, the crucial unit was the 15th Transport and Communication Wing (*15 Vervoer en Verbindungswing*). Originally established in 1948 from the former 169th Wing, it comprised No 20 and 21 Squadrons and operated Percival Pembroke, Douglas DC-4 and DC-6, and Fairchild C-119G Packet transports. In 1950, the Wing moved from Evere to Groenvald Camp, outside Melsbroek, and four years later it was reinforced through the addition of No 40 Squadron, also equipped with C-119s.

In order to replace worn out Packets, in 1971, Belgium placed an order for 12 C-130Hs. The first arrived in Belgium on 25 July 1972. Following their arrival, this and all other aircraft were sent to Marshalls workshop in Cambridge, UK, where they received the same 'South-East Asia' camouflage pattern as applied on many C-130s exported to other foreign customers. Thus, it was only when the first re-painted Hercules returned to Melsbroek, on 16 May 1973, that the No 20 and No 21 Squadrons were officially declared as operational on the type. It is notable that by this time

Table 6: C 130Hs of the 15th Wing Belgian Air Force

Construction Number	US FY-serial	Belgian Air Force Serial
4455	71-1797	CH-01
4460	71-1798	CH-02
4461	71-1799	CH-03
4467	71-1800	CH-04
4470	71-1801	CH-05
4473	71-1802	CH-06
4474	71-1803	CH-07
4478	71-1804	CH-08
4479	71-1805	CH-09
4481	71-1806	CH-10
4482	71-1807	CH-11
4483	71-1808	CH-12

Colonel Phillipe Erulin

Phillipe Erulin was born on 5 July 1932 into a family with very strong military traditions: his grandfather fought and was killed in the First World War, while his father's grave could be found amongst the dead French soldiers in Indochina: he was killed in 1951.

The future commander of 2e REP enlisted into the prestigious Saint-Cyr military academy in 1952. Two years later he achieved the rank of second lieutenant. Between 1955 and 1961 Erulin fought in Algeria, and during his involvement in the battle of Algiers he became targeted by the French press, apparently for brutality against FLN insurgency.

After his second tour of Algeria, for the above reasons, he was seconded to become an instructor at the Infantry Academy in Montpellier. Later he was sent to one of the garrisons in Alsace, and overseas to the Diego Suarez base in Madagascar.

In 1970, completing relevant courses, he was assigned the post of chief instructor in 2e REP. In July 1976 he took over the command of 2e REP for a period of two years, leading his men to the remarkable completion of Operation *Leopard* in Kolwezi in May 1978. He was assigned to the staff of the air force, where he took charge of coordination of the airborne troops. Awarded the Legion of Honour, the *Croix de Guerre*, and holder of four citations, he died in September 1979 of a cardiac arrest.

Colonel Phillipe Erulin, commander of 2e REP in 1978. (Foreign Legion release, via Daniel Kowalczuk)

A group of Belgian Para-Commandos as seen in Zaire, in May 1978. In addition to their distinctively coloured berets (maroon in this case, denoting the 1st Regiment), notable are their camouflage smocks and trousers similar to the Denison-style British-pattern and FN/FAL assault rifles. (Albert Grandolini Collection)

these two units were re-located to the military side of the Brussels/Zaventem Airport, and serviced in the workshops of the national airline Sabena. As of 1977-1978, other than 12 C-130Hs (listed in Table 6), the 15th Wing also operated two Boeing 727 airliners, several Hawker-Siddeley HS.748s, Dassault Mystère 20s, and a Fairchild Merlin IIIA: in May 1978, the commander of this unit, Colonel Alaine Blueme, could call upon ten C-130s and two Boeing 727s.

Belgian Para-Commandos

The Belgian Para Commando Regiment had changed its equipment little from that of Operation *Red Dragon* 14 years earlier in Stanleyville, Congo. Each battalion of the regiment wore its own distinctively coloured beret (1st – maroon; 2nd – green and 3rd – maroon), and the 1st Battalion's soldiers also sometimes wore a metal SAS badge, commemorating the roots of Belgian Para Commandos with the British special forces. Shoulder epaulettes were red with blue edges, the actual rank in silver, and overall, the Belgian Paras' uniform was still heavily influenced by British design. Smocks were almost identical to the Denison-style British-pattern, with webbing belts the same as the British 1937 design. On this occasion, disembarking straight from their aircraft into a less hostile environment than the French before them, the Belgians hardly had to wear their helmets for protection – those used by the Belgian Paras being the very popular West German M71 helmet – putting on their berets instead.

The standard personal weapon of the Para Commando in 1978 was the NATO 7.62 mm calibre FN-FAL assault rifle (including the folding stock M3 "para" version), made in Belgium and arguably, after chocolates and beer, the most famous ever export product of Belgian industry.

There are some photos showing Belgian soldiers in Kolwezi with the famous, though obsolete, Vigneron SMG. As with their French comrades with the MAT-49, the Belgian elite soldiers saw no the reason to hurry with replacing a reliable and combat proven weapon with the more modern assault rifles.

Table 7: Organization of the Belgian Para-Commando Regiment, 1977-1978

Unit	Elements	Notes
1st Battalion	11th, 13th and 21st Companies	
2nd Battalion	14th Company	
3rd Battalion	15th & 17th Companies	

Safari Club: Inter-African Forces

Equipped and supervised by the French, and supported by Belgium and the USA, five countries allied with France provided contingents from their military forces for the intervention in Zaire of 1978. All the countries in question were former French colonies, with rather small military forces. More importantly, their intervention was coordinated by a covert multi-national organization called the Safari Club: an anti-Communist alliance including France, Egypt, Morocco, Iran, and Saudi Arabia.[27]

The strongest amongst them was the military of Morocco, totalling about 81,000 officers and other ranks as of the mid-1970s, with an eclectic mixture of relatively modern equipment sourced

AML-90 armoured cars of the Senegalese Army. (Mark Lepko Collection)

from both East and West. The Royal Moroccan Air force had about 6,000 officers and other ranks, and operated about 60 combat aircraft. In addition to deploying its contingent to Zaire of 1978, Morocco maintained a contingent of 8,000 troops in Mauritania, while the majority of its armed forces were continuously involved in fighting a large- and well-organized insurgency in Western Sahara.

Gabon had a small military of only about 950 officers and other ranks; whilst the army of Senegal totalled about 6,000 men; Togo's military included only about 2,950 personnel; and the military of Ivory Coast totalled about 4,500, with an air force that had about 200 officers and other ranks that operated about 20 transport aircraft and helicopters.

CHAPTER 4
ANGOLAN POWDER KEG

Although living in exile, the surviving Katangese Gendarmes never lost hope of reigniting the secessionist movement in Katanga. Through the late 1960s and early 1970s, some soldiers amongst them continued serving as 'guns for hire' – now on contracts to the Portuguese colonial authorities in Angola. Starting in 1967, they were formed into five small battalions known as 'Black Arrows' that served on COIN operations. During the following years, they primarily fought against the insurgents of such nationalist Angolan movements like the Movement for the Liberation of Angola (*Movimento Popular de Libertação de Angola*, MPLA), led by Agustino Neto; the National Union for the Total Independence of Angola (*Uniao Nacional para a Independència Total de Angola*, UNITA); and the National Front for the Liberation of Angola (*Frente Nacional de Libertação de Angola*, FNLA), led by Holden Roberto and supported by Mobutu.

Gradually, the Portuguese expanded this force to about 2,500 men and officially recognized them as one of six 'loyal native African forces', the so-called *Leais* ('the Loyal ones'). The Black Arrows were re-organized into five 'battalions', each totalling between 300 and 350 fighters and including two or three companies. As the movement continued to grow, it was reinforced through the recruitment of its future leader, Nathaniel Mbumba, in 1968. Furthermore, with some support of the Portuguese – who remained staunch enemies of Mobutu until their withdrawal – it began changing its ideology: a year later, it severed ties with traditional Lunda kings ('Mwaant Yaws') of Katanga due to internal differences, and changed its designation into the *Front National pour la Libération du Congo* (National Front for the Liberation of the Congo, FNLC).

Together with other Portuguese forces, the FNLC proved highly effective in de-facto destroying the MPLA and greatly weakening the FNLA, in 1971-1972.

Alliance with the MPLA

However, in April 1974, the Carnation Revolution – a coup of leftist officers in Lisbon – caused a fundamental change in the foreign policy of Portugal. The new government ordered an end to all offensive operations in Angola and then announced its intention to withdraw from this territory. The result was one of utter chaos: although the Portuguese military was still present in Angola, and the local bases were used for the withdrawal of military contingents and colonists from Mozambique, the Portuguese had let the FNLA, followed by the MPLA and the UNITA into Luanda in late 1974. Before long, differences between the three moments erupted in a civil war. Interrupted by numerous cease-fires negotiated by the Portuguese, this conflict was gradually won by the MPLA, which managed to turn most of the native population in its favour. Neto's underestimated movement thus won control over the future capital of the country months before the Portuguese withdrew.

Nevertheless, the MPLA was barely holding out and lacked the troop strength necessary to bring more of Angola, other than Luanda and its immediate surroundings, under its control. Control of the capital, but also of remaining territory of Angola was of critical importance if the MPLA was to be recognized as the new government of the independent country by the Organization of the African Unity (OAU), once the Portuguese were to officially withdraw, in November 1975.

With the majority of its 'combatants' consisting of poorly trained and poorly disciplined youths – like the group visible in this photo – the MPLA was critically short on any kind of troops as of 1974-1975. (Albert Grandolini Collection)

FAZ officers discussing the situation with a group of white mercenaries during the advance into northern Angola. (Albert Grandolini Collection)

It was under such conditions that on 17 December 1974 the MPLA and the FNLC reached a fateful agreement: the Tigers had promised to fight on the side of the MPLA/FAPLA should this come under attack from the FNLA or UNITA. In return, the MPLA promised to support the FNLC in its struggle against Mobutu. In this fashion, the MPLA and the FAPLA – which had no serious war-fighting capability as of late 1974 – were reinforced by four small but experienced and disciplined battalions, including at least 2000 well-trained, battle-hardened Katangan troops.[28]

During the following months, the MPLA further managed to secure Cuban support – in the form of a sizeable Military Assistance Mission – and place orders for large arms shipments from the USSR. However, it was obvious that it would take months for these to arrive, and at least as long for Cuban advisors to train enough members of the MPLA's emerging military wing (and the future military of Angola) – the People's Armed Forces of Liberation of Angola (*Forcas Armadas Populares de Libertação de Angola*, FAPLA): within the context of Angola of 1975, such assets were worth their weight in gold.

The reason for this was that upon realising that the MPLA had established itself in power in Luanda, the US, French and Zairean supported FNLA, and the South African supported UNITA created a coalition with the intention

The Union of Aerial Transports (*Union de Transports Aériens*, UTA) was a French airline that operated from 1963 until 1994. While privately owned, it had a history of flying long-range routes and of close cooperation with the French government. Starting in the 1960s, it replaced most older types with the Douglas DC-8, the fleet of which eventually grew to 24 aircraft (including at least two freighter variants). Three of these were used to fly Legionnaires of the 2e REP from Solenzara AB on Corsica, to N'Djili IAP, on 18 May 1978: this artwork shows one of the company's DC-8-62s confirmed as involved in transporting paras of the 2e REP to Zaire: F-BNLE. (Artwork by Tom Cooper)

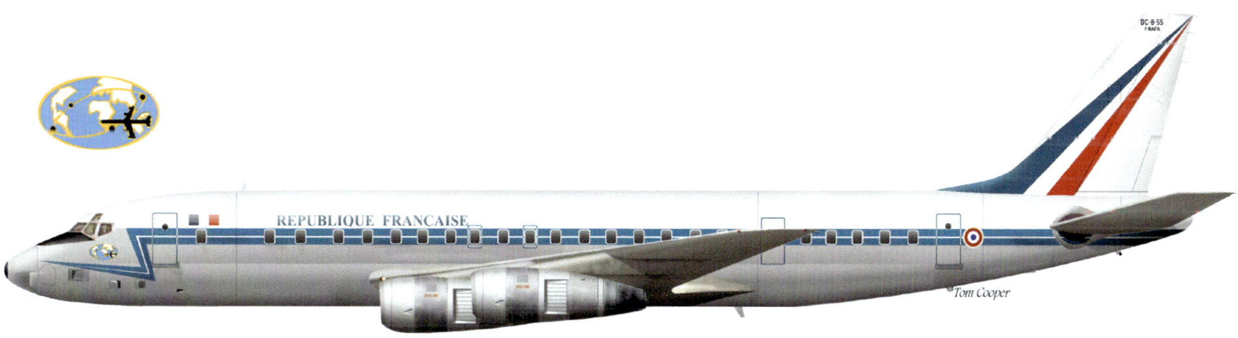

COTAM was the acronym for the Military Air Transport Command of the French Air Force. Established in February 1962, by the mid-1980s this branch grew to a total of 28 squadrons, including ten flying fixed-wing aircraft, before it was disbanded in March 1994. Two of COTAM's transport squadrons (*Escadron de Transport*, ET) flew airliners for transport purposes: one of these was ET 3/60 Estrél, which operated DC-8s of a number of variants since 1966. This artwork shows the first DC-8-55 operated by ET 3/60: F-RAFA.

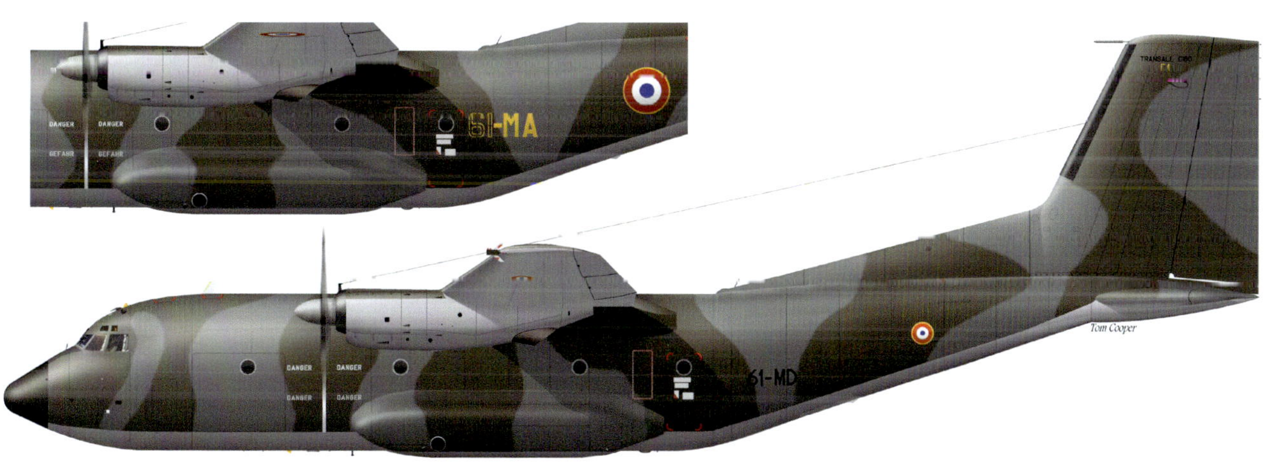

Developed and manufactured as a joint venture between France and Germany, the C.160F Transall was a version for the French Air Force, 50 of which were manufactured starting in 1967. The type saw quite some action in relation to Zaire: in April 1977, 12 C.160s were used to airlift Moroccan troops and equipment to Zaire, while in May 1978 three were deployed to N'Djili IAP in support of the 2e REP's assault of Kolwezi. All the aircraft in question were operated by three squadrons of the Transport Wing 61 (*61e Escadre de Transport*), based at Orléans/Bricy AB. While retaining their original camouflage pattern consisting of dark grey and dark green on top surfaces and sides, and aluminium on undersurfaces, their codes were initially applied in yellow and quite large digits, but by May 1978 these were replaced with less obvious codes applied in black only. Shown are Transalls F1/61-MA (inset) and F4/61-MD (the latter is known to have participated in the Operation *Leopard*). (Artwork by Tom Cooper)

The FAZA acquired three DHC-5s in the early 1970s, and at least two of these were operational during the two Shaba Wars. While held back by a Zairian general who seems to have misappropriated them for his own purposes in 1977, they saw intensive involvement in operations in 1978. All three aircraft were painted in a variant of the US Air Force's 'South East Asia' camouflage pattern, including tan (FS30219), light green (FS34102), and dark olive green (FS34079) on top surfaces, and light grey (FS36622) on undersurfaces. Registrations for the three aircraft were 9T-TBA, 9T-TBB and 9T-TBC. Contrary to C-130Hs, they all received fin flashes. (Artwork by Tom Cooper)

The FAZA acquired a total of seven C-130Hs, and these received registrations ranging from 9T-TCA to 9T-TCF. Six were still intact as of 18 May 1978, of which five were available, and all of these five flew operations in support of the 2e REP's mission to Kolwezi. Subsequently, they were included in the international airbridge run by multiple Western air forces between diverse bases abroad, N'Djili IAP, Kamina AB, Lubumbashi and Kolwezi airports. All were painted in the US Air Force's 'South East Asia' camouflage pattern, including tan (FS30219), light green (FS34102), and dark olive green (FS34079) on top surfaces, and light grey (FS36622) on undersurfaces. (Artwork by Tom Cooper

As of the mid-1970s, C-130Hs of the 15th Wing of the Belgian Air Force were all painted in the US Air Force's 'South East Asia' camouflage pattern, including tan, light green, and dark olive green on top surfaces, and light grey on undersurfaces. However, because these were applied in the UK, it is possible that their exact shades were slightly different to those applied on other exported examples. All wore big black codes on the fin, repeated below the cockpit. Inset is shown the insignia of the 15th Wing: the head of a Sioux Indian on a light blue shield outlined red and dark blue. The head-dress had black and white feathers and a white headband with black triangles over the forehead. (Artworks by Tom Cooper)

This is a reconstruction of one of five MB.326BG Sukisas known to have been destroyed by the FNLC at Kolwezi 'Main', on 13 May 1978. Notable are the 'Nile Valley'-style camouflage pattern (developed by the Egyptian Air Force in the early 1970s) applied in the same tan, light green, and dark olive green on top surfaces, and light grey on undersurfaces – as on C-130s and DHC-5s – and a single-piece cockpit canopy. Underwing drop tanks were carried almost always, but were deleted in this case to better show the machine-gun pod (with one M2 Browning .50cal/12.7mm machine gun and its ammunition): this was painted entirely in dark olive green, and installed on inboard underwing station. Pods containing reconnaissance cameras had a very similar form, but a stubbier nose. (Artwork by Tom Cooper)

A reconstruction of the MB.326BG Sukisa known to have been damaged in an emergency landing – the precise details of which remain unknown – during II Shaba War. By that time, the camouflage pattern began showing traces of exposure to the elements and the relatively intensive operations of 1977 and 1978; nevertheless, the entire fleet retained not only the outside wing-tip fuel tanks, but also fin-tips and tips of horizontal stabilisers painted in dayglo orange. This aircraft is shown together with an underwing drop tank and the two primary types of rocket pods used in 1977 (lower right corner): LAU-32 and Matra F2 (nowadays Thales LRF2) – both for SNEB 68mm rockets. (Artwork by Tom Cooper

Two MB.326GBs that were badly damaged at Kolwezi were subsequently sent to Italy for repairs where they re-appeared in the period 1981-1983. The aircraft in question emerged wearing the same camouflage pattern as originally, but applied with even softer lower borders, and equipped with a two-part cockpit hood. Notable is that their camouflage pattern was extended over their wing-tip fuel tanks. (Artwork by Tom Cooper)

Mirage 5Ms (or 'M5Ms' according to the title applied on their forward fuselages prior to delivery) acquired by Zaire wore a unique camouflage pattern consisting of the same bronze green (*gris vert foncé*) as used on aircraft of the French Air Force in the 1970s, but combined with apple green, on top surfaces. These were applied along the lines of the standard camouflage pattern. Undersides appear to have been painted in aluminium colour. The aircraft wore their national insignia on the fin and on top and bottom surfaces of the wing. Typical armament consisted of two 200kg or 250kg bombs installed in tandem under the centreline. Some of the Mirages operated from Kamina AB in May 1978 were sighted while equipped with drop tanks painted in worn out brick red colour: it is possible that the protective cover of these was never properly removed. (Artwork by Tom Cooper)

A reconstruction of a FAZA SA.316B Alouette III sighted on multiple occasions during the II Shaba War, in May 1978. The construction number of this helicopter should have been 1359, but its original serial number remains unclear. Delivered in a much darker green colour, by 1978 it appeared as shown here: painted in grey-green overall and wearing the code 9T-HT1. Flown by Zairian and French pilots FAZA's Alouettes saw intensive action during the Shaba II, sometimes serving as forward air controllers, and directing air strikes by Mirages. (Artwork by Tom Cooper)

A reconstruction of the SA.330C Puma of the FAZA registered as 9T-HP6: this helicopter was used as a VIP-transport and was often seen carrying Mobutu around the country. While painted in green-grey overall, contrary to most of other Zairian Pumas, it received no black colour on the engine cowling behind the exhaust. Instead, it wore the official crest of Zaire on the cabin side: this consisted of a Leopard, Olive Branch, Ivory, and two spears, and the inscription 'Justice, Paix, Travail' – applied in yellow-gold and black colours. (Artwork by Tom Cooper)

A reconstruction of one of about a dozen M3 half-tracks still operated by the FAZ as of the mid-1970s. While retaining its original colour of olive drab overall, the vehicle received wide stripes in sand or tan down the superstructure. A few of these had been deployed to Shaba in 1977 and 1978, perhaps by elements of the Kamanyola Division, but it remains unknown how much action – if any – they saw. (Artwork by David Bocquelet)

The FAZ acquired a total of 220 AML-60s and AML-90s during the first half of the 1970s. Up to two dozen were knocked out by enemy fire or mines, or abandoned and left behind during the ill-fated adventures in Angola of late 1975, while the majority of survivors were concentrated within the 1st Armoured Brigade. Nevertheless, at least two squadrons were present in Shaba as of 1977, and proved decisive during the FAZ counteroffensive. In 1978, four AML-60s and AML-90s were captured by the FNLC, which pressed them into service, but quickly lost two in the first clash with the 2e REP, including this AML-90. As far as is known, all the FAZ's AMLs were painted in green overall: many wore 'personal' names or various other insignia on their turrets, but none are known for the AML-90s deployed in the Kolwezi area. (Artwork by David Bocquelet)

Following the success of Colonel Ikuku Moboto's 122nd Battalion of the 12th Brigade Kamanyola Division during attack on the train station in Lufupa, in 1977, many of the AMLs operated by that unit received the title 'Serpent de Railes' applied to the side of their turret, in commemoration of the nickname 'Railroad Snake' given to Ukuku by the defeated FNLC. At least one of the AML-60s decorated in this fashion was captured by the FNLC during the attack on Kolwezi, a year later: however, the vehicle appears to have been abandoned by the insurgents without seeing further action during Shaba II. (Artwork by David Bocquelet)

Right: Caporal Chef (Master Corporal) *4e Compagnie – 2e Régiment Étranger de Parachutistes*, Kolwezi, May 1978.
Unlike the other legionaries who jumped on Kolwezi, from the outset, the 4e Compagniewas dressed in the TTA 47 combat dress, characterized by the 'lizard' camouflage pattern and its spartan design. The need for high mobility can be measured by the simplicity of this experienced Legionnaire's equipment: the steel helmet has been set aside in favour of the legion's green beret which bears the insignia of the French paratroopers. He also wears TAP 50/53 equipment; on the canvas belt, he carries a fabric holster for the MAC 50 pistol and a very useful combat knife. The bag on the top of the suspender was usually used to carry a first aid kit. His rifle is a MAS FR F1, which was to prove quite effective in Kolwezi. The latest versions of this weapon fire NATO's 7.62 mm, but the weapon seen here is still sized for the French 7.5 mm calibre. (artwork by Anderson Subtil)

Below: Caporal (Corporal) CEA (*compagnie d'éclairage et d'appui*) *2e Régiment Étranger de Parachutistes* Kinshasa/Kolwezi, May 1978.This legionnaire is seen here shortly before joining the C-130 Hercules that would take him to the legendary leap over Kolwezi. This legionnaire of the 2e REP is equipped with a US T-10 parachute borrowed from local airborne troops, while the remainder of his clothing and equipment are all of French origin. He wears the then-recent Satin 300 *'tenue de combat'* (combat uniform), which would be characteristic of French intervention forces in the following years, although the set of suspenders, belt and bags were still of the TAP 50/53 pattern as had been used in Algeria. The blue cloth just visible around the left shoulder serves to identify the company. His head is well protected by a 1956 Modèle helmet, suitable for airborne actions; his boots are of the conventional type of the French Army. Armament consists of a MAC 50 pistol in 9mm Parabellum and a MAT-49 submachinegun, also in the same calibre, a weapon much appreciated by the Legion since its involvement in Indochina. (artwork by Anderson Subtil)

Left: Senior Officer, Centre D'entrainement des Troupes Aéroportées, Kinshasa, 1978.
Supposedly of Belgian origin, the Leopard-spot camouflage pattern of the *Forces Armée Zaïroise* (FAZ) began to be used in the new nation from 1973, in a rare example of camouflage adopted more for show than the ability to hide. Although in use in Libya and Chad, the Zaire pattern was differentiated by the use of black dots on a vertically striped background in light green and brown and was most likely adopted after the direct interference of Mobutu, who used the title 'The Leopard' and was often seen wearing leopard fur cap. The camouflage, however, was never a universal issue, being restricted to units considered as elite; mainly to the parachutists, commandos and the Kamanyola Division, along with other standards, like the French lizard pattern. Conventional units, and the presidential guard, wore olive uniforms.
This senior officer, probably a major or lieutenant-colonel, seen during a presidential inspection at the *Center d'entrainement des Troupes Aéroportées* (CETA, Airborne Troops Training Centre), near the International Airport of Kinshasa, where French officers trained one of the battalions of the 31st Brigade of Parachutists, is dressed in 'leopard-spots', and also wears the characteristic red beret of the parachutists of Zaire, a colour that is repeated in the other eye-catching insignia of a senior officer. The parachute wings are fastened to the right pocket of the shirt, and have a gold finish indicating that they belong to an instructor. The leather belt was most likely imported from Belgium, also the origin of the ceremonial sabre held in his right hand. (artwork by Anderson Subtil)

A relatively rare, colour photograph of the first MB.326BG manufactured for the Congo/Zaire, showing the aircraft in its original livery – including outsides of the wing-tip fuel tanks, fin- and stabilizer-tips in dayglo orange. (Milpix/Martin Hornliman Collection)

One of FAZA's MB.326BGs repaired in Italy in the early 1980s was this example, FG-461. While next to nothing had changed in terms of the camouflage pattern and markings, notable are the two-piece canopy and camouflage colours applied on the wing-tip fuel tank. (Milpix/Martin Hornliman Collection)

Right-hand view of the same aircraft, this time without any parts covered by tarpaulin. (Milpix/Martin Hornliman Collection)

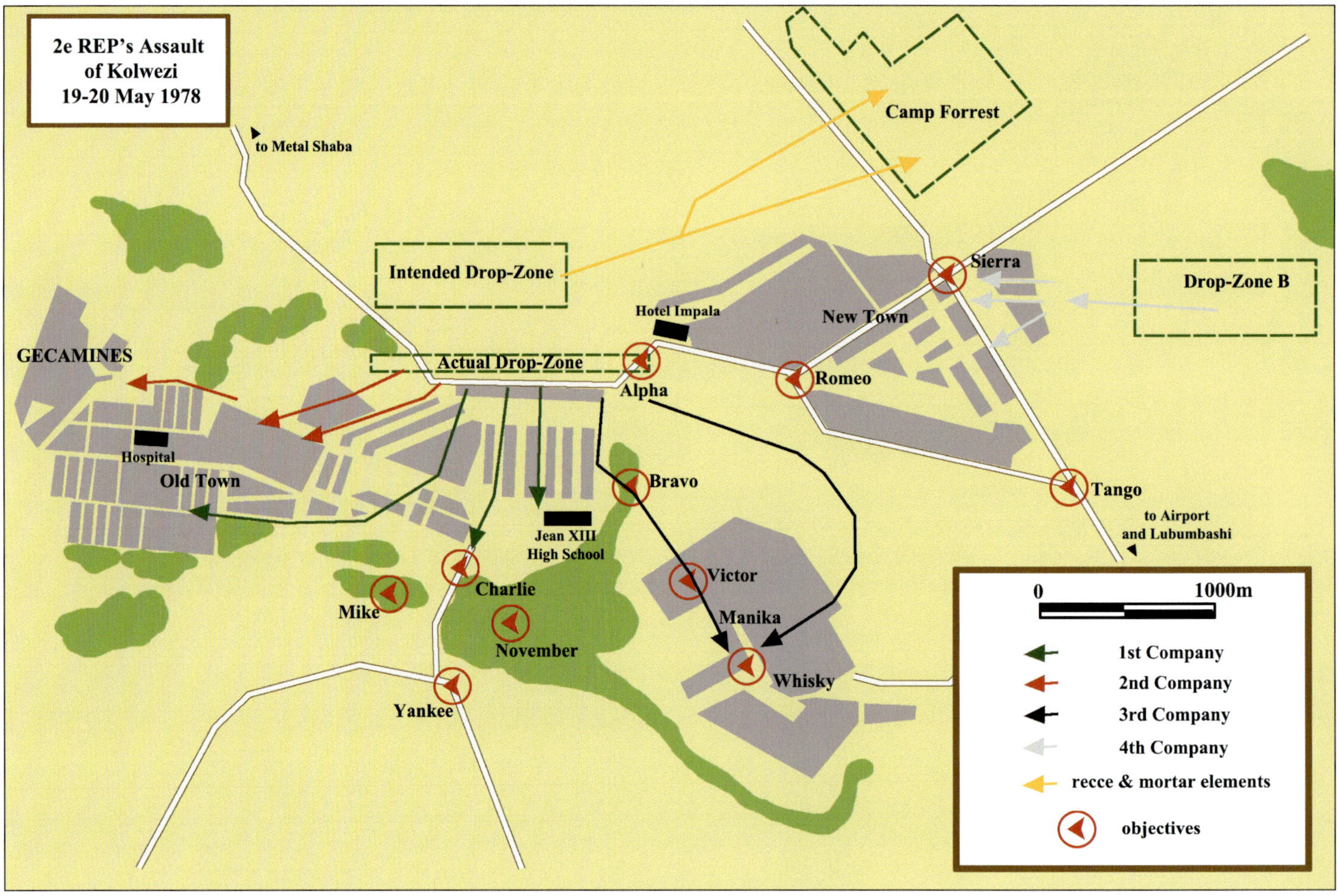

Map of the 2e REP's jump and assault into Kolwezi, on 19 and 20 May 1978. (Map by Tom Cooper)

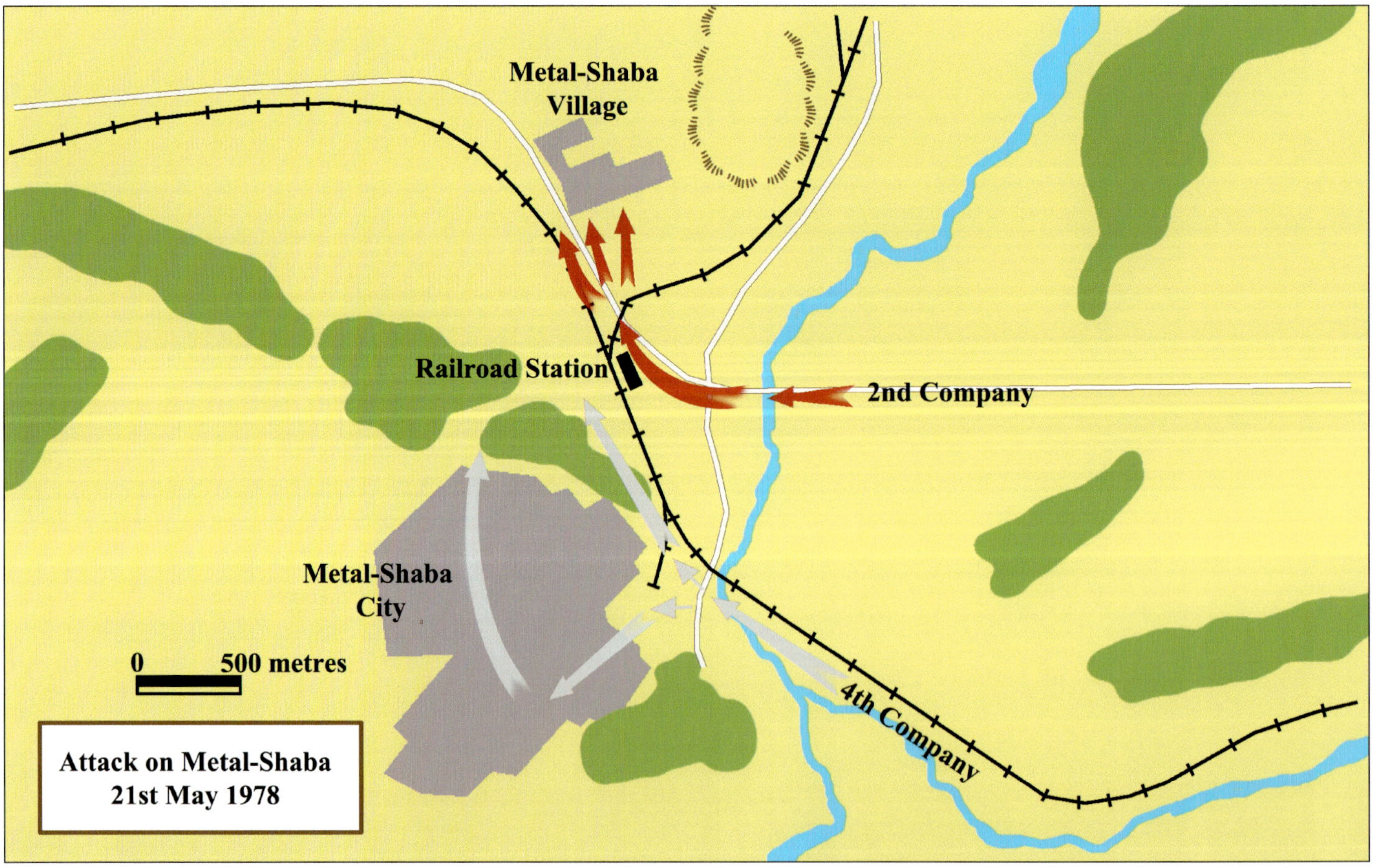

Map of the advance by the (reinforced) 2nd and 4th Companies 2e REP on the Metal-Shaba complex (north-west of Kolwezi), on 21 May 1978, which resulted in the biggest clash with the FNLC and heaviest single loss of the Legionnaires. (Map by Tom Cooper)

A white mercenary with an AML-60 'donated' by the FAZ and a group of UNITA insurgents in Angola in 1975. (Albert Grandolini Collection)

of wrestling the control of the country, and its capital, from the MPLA – and that before the Portuguese had left. Furthermore, Mobutu and the French external intelligence agency – the Directorate-General for External Security (*Direction Générale de la Sécurité Extérieure*, DGSE) – decided to also provide support for the armed group of separatists in the Cabinda enclave, an oil-rich part of Angola north of western Zaire, organized as the organized as the Front for the Liberation of the Enclave of Cabinda (*Frente para a Libertação do Enclave de Cabinda*, FLEC). Overall the FAZ – which had previously seen combat deployments in a number of minor conflicts – like its deployment in Nigeria, where it helped end the Bifran Secessionist War, in 1970, or in Burundi, where it helped restore the local government, in 1971 – became involved in its largest combat operation ever: a military intervention in Angola in 1975.

The Rout in Angola

In the summer of 1975 the FAZ deployed its 7th and 14th Parachute Battalions, and a supporting force including two squadrons of AML-60s and AML-90s and artillery – equalling a light brigade in total – to reinforce Roberto Holden's FNLA for an invasion of northern Angola. After a relatively quick advance, this force reached a point only 35 kilometres north of Luanda. The South Africans had meanwhile invaded southern Angola and then launched a rapid advance, reaching a point about 200 kilometres south of Luanda, while UNITA won a series of battles in the east of the country. It was only in the course of several de-facto 'last ditch' actions run simultaneously on multiple fronts, that the Cubans, the MPLA/FAPLA and the Katangan Tigers eventually managed to stop all these advances into Angola in October and November 1975. Indeed, in the Cabinda enclave, the Cubans and the FAPLA completely defeated the combined FAZ-FLEC force, reinforced by a sizeable group of foreign mercenaries. Furthermore, during their campaigns run in northern Angola between November 1975 and February 1976, the Cubans and the FAPLA then soundly defeated the FNLA and the FAZ: whatever was left of Mobutu's 'crack' paratroopers and their allies, disintegrated in face of enemy firepower, with only half of the Zairean troops deployed inside northern Angola ever accounted for again, while the rest deserted and never reported back to their units.[29]

Discouraged by developments in the north, but especially by the growing international criticism and pressure, the South Africans then decided to cease their intervention and withdraw from Angola, leaving UNITA on its own, in February 1976. The MPLA

An ex-FAZ M-3 APC, knocked out while operated by white mercenaries in support of the FNLA (the military wing of which was named 'ELNA', a title which in turn was written in big white letters on the front hull of this unlucky vehicle), in Angola of November 1975. (Albert Grandolini Collection)

– meanwhile reinforced by the arrival of at least 35,000 Cuban troops and immense shipments of arms purchased from the USSR – thus establishing itself in power in the country. Led by the rather underestimated Agostinho Neto, the government of the nascent nation quickly signed a peace treaty with the Congo-Brazzaville. Similarly, Neto agreed with Mobutu to cease supporting any kind of dissident organisations: nevertheless, greatly appreciating the help the FNLC had provided at the times of greatest need, he could not but fulfil his promise to Mbumba. Correspondingly, he continued supporting the Katangese (but also a few other, smaller Zairian opposition groups) with arms and supplies, just as Mobutu continued supporting the FNLA and the FLEC.

Reform of the FNLC

This is how it came to be that the former Katangese Gendarmes, who once used to bitterly oppose leftist Lumumbists and the Simbas of the Congo, now ended-up taking on the MPLA's leftist ideology and planning a new war against Mobutu's clearly 'pro-Western' government in Kinshasa. On the contrary, the Katangese movement in Angola subsequently broke all its links to the legacy of the Katangan secession movement of 1960-1963. Instead, a leftist influence began to be felt – also in the form of Mbumba forcing his cadre to start using the term 'comrade'. Whatever was left of the openly 'pro-Western' Katangese Army of the former 'State of Katanga', thus converted itself into a leftist proxy of the Angolan government.

MPLA activists raising their flag – the new national flag of Angola – in November 1975. Following the example of the MPLA, the FNLC began adapting its ideology towards the political left. (Albert Grandolini Collection)

Indeed, knowing that Mobutu never ceased supporting the FNLA and the FLEC – both of which remained active in northern Angola and the Cabinda enclave between 1976 and 1978 – Neto quickly grew fed up of the Zairian strongman. While keeping the Cubans (probably the Soviets too) out of the loop about the FNLC's designs for an invasion of Zaire, and despite the massive Cuban military presence in Angola (and this playing a crucial role in the military build-up of the FAPLA), there is no evidence for the FNLC ever receiving any substantial training from Cuban advisors. On the contrary, it seems that Havana was quite incensed about not being informed of the intentions of the Angolan and Katangan leaders with regards to an invasion of Zaire. Unsurprisingly, there is no evidence at the time of writing for the Cubans having provided any kind of military support to the Katangese during the two Shaba Wars.[30]

Table 8: FNLC's Military Organization, 1975-1978

Unit	Notes
1st Battalion	CO General Mufu; involved in Shaba I
2nd Battalion	involved in Shaba II
3rd Battalion	
4th Battalion	
5th Battalion	
6th Battalion	est. 1978
7th Battalion	est. 1978; involved in Shaba II
8th Battalion	est. 1978
9th Battalion	est. 1978
10th Battalion	est. 1978
11th Battalion	est. 1978

FNLC Regulars

During the two Shaba Wars of 1977 and 1978, the FNLC attempted to provide its troops with uniforms and equipment that were as homogenous as possible – even if this proved extremely hard to achieve. Old uniforms of the Katangan Army and ANC commandos, from the mid-1960s, were worn out during earlier campaigns and their stocks were dramatically decreased since 1967. The Portuguese then tried their best to provide uniforms to its allies. The problem was, colonial regulars themselves were facing supply chain difficulties, caused by overstretching of the Portuguese Army's logistic abilities and limited budgets.

The FNLC, during its support for Portuguese in Angola, was uniformed in standard Portuguese Army camouflage uniforms, based on the French 1950-pattern, together with standard infantry field caps, the FNLC received significant number of dark green Paras berets.

During the civil war in Angola, the FNLC, as the MPLA's ally, was slowly re-equipped with the Cuban supplied stores, with Cuban style plain uniforms being issued in large numbers. At the time of "Shaba I," the FNLC looked more like a rag-tag guerrilla army, to the dismay of the local population who expected a smart looking regular army, liberating Katanga from Mobutu oppression. However, a few battalions formed significantly earlier, maintained the appearance of regulars, thanks to individual quarter masters' connections to the Portuguese command before 1974.

The ranks of the ex-Gendarmes, up to 1967, were parallel to the *Force Publique* in pre-independent Congo, later mirrored during the formation of the *Forces Armees Katangaises*. In Angola, trained and organised by the Portuguese, they followed the rank order of Portuguese colonial troops, this basically prevailed up to the Shaba Wars, with the notable exception of adding Eastern Block style "political commissars" – officers indoctrinating soldiers and keeping an eye on any discontent, caused by FNLC leadership and its sudden changes of allegiance.

The weaponry of the FNLC in 1978 was a different issue altogether. Counting the number of small arms available after the

A meeting of the FNLC's leadership in one of its bases in Angola. (FNLC release)

The 'Women's Battalion' of the FNLC. This battalion, operational by 1977, was completely staffed by female combatants. (FNLC release)

withdrawal of the Portuguese in 1974, the FNLC could cherry pick from many sources. West German G3 assault rifles were very popular from 1970, when they were supplied by the Portuguese. Ammunition for them became scarce in 1975-76, so the FNLC reluctantly re-armed with AK-47 assault rifles and their copies from various Eastern Bloc countries, especially Communist China.

FNLC Loyalists

Apart from the notoriously pro-FNLC District of Manika in Kolwezi, nowhere else was to provide any organised local support for the rebels. In Manika itself, the FNLC recruited several hundred 'auxiliaries', determined to prove their loyalty to the expected new government. These were the very people accused of the majority of killings of the white population and "pro-Mobutu" locals in Kolwezi. FNLC supporters in the Shaba Wars had been a very important factor for the ex-Gendarmes. At first, they provided crucial intelligence about FAZ strength in the area in 1977, however they were an "elite" amongst loyalists, who were not large in numbers, up to the point when Mobutu summarily punished alleged FNLC sympathisers in Shaba province. This practice practically "marched" hundreds of young Lunda into the arms of the FNLC.

In terms of thier equipment and uniform, they did not differ noticeably from the civilians. A few dozens of FNLC "loyalists" used FAZ stock seized from a depot in Kolwezi, and adopted some FAZ uniforms garments in an ad hoc fashion, but there is no evidence of that being in pursuit of some order or following any pattern of homogenic locally recruited units, uniformed the same way.

FNLC loyalists in Kolwezi were commanded by regular officers of that organisation. Significantly larger than the "regular" FNLC was the number of politically motivated members, well aware of Mobutu's atrocities and willing to take the "socialist" path – if the FNLC succeeded.

Weapons were self-supplied by improvisation, and followed the "everybody for themselves" rule. The FNLC provided some small arms, taken during Shaba I from retreating FAZ units, and stashed some in locations in the Kolwezi region, or given to the "loyalists" to keep in safe houses. During the massacres committed against European civilians, FNLC supporters used some primative weapons, such as machetes, and possibly even ritual spears and arrows, as suggested by some details of the wounds inflicted upon the dead hostages.

The number of active FNLC local "auxiliary" force never reached as high as 500 insurgents, with far less than that routinely armed.

CHAPTER 5
I SHABA WAR

The conflict that eventually became known as 'Shaba I' or the 'I Shaba War' was a short war triggered by an invasion of the Zairian province of Shaba by about a brigade-strong group of FNLC insurgents in 1977, with the intention of first turning the local population against Mobutu, and then trying to persuade local FAZ units to change sides and 'join the revolution'. The overall goal of the FNLC was to topple Mobutu – preferably in cooperation with other opposition groups – and create a socialist state. At least according to Mbumba, the FNLC had no intention to separate Shaba from Zaire: indeed, he distanced himself outright from a 'Tshombist-style' breakaway. Actually, it seems that as of 1977 the FNLC was desperate to 'make a statement' because of the growing impatience of its leader with regards to the movement's increasingly unclear status in Angola. As it turned out, if it was not for the help provided by several of Mobutu's foreign allies, the insurgency could have achieved at least some of its aims.

Invasion

During the night from 7 to 8 March 1977, a total of about 2,000 FNLC troops moved out of their forward camps at Cazombo, Tshimbima, and Luso in Angola (most were less than 10 kilometres from the Zairian border), and crossed the border before moving in a northern and eastern direction. Their plan was relatively simple: one battalion with three companies (Company K/11, L/12 and M/14) was to move north and take Dilolo, Sandoa and Kapanga; another battalion (with three of their own, plus one extra company) was to follow in the wake of the first, but then turn east in Sandoa and take Bukuma. Together, these two units were then to attack

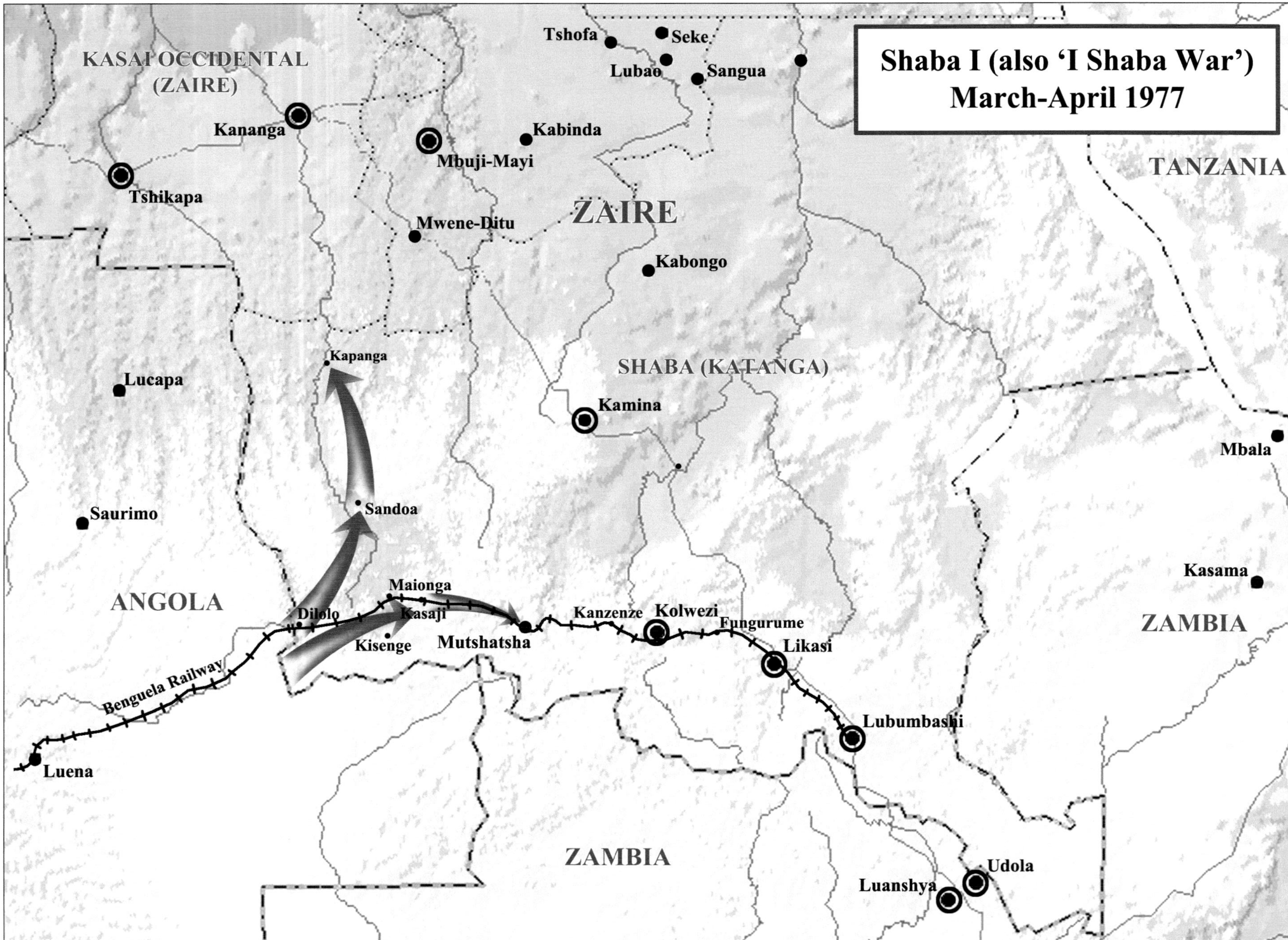

Map of the main routes of advance used by the FNLC during the I Shaba War in March-April 1977. (Map by Tom Cooper)

FNLC insurgents on the advance in Zaire in April 1977. (FNLC release)

'old guard' of the Katangan Gendarmes, who commanded the 1st Battalion) – and travelling on foot (some on bicycles), the advance initially proceeded very well. The FNLC first took Dilolo and then secured Kasaji, around 1330hrs local time on 8 March, before continuing to their actual objectives: Kamina and Kolwezi. Underway there, they sought to capture as many trucks as possible, in order to accelerate their march, but also to recruit additional combatants. Meanwhile, the 2nd Battalion FNLC advanced via Kasaji, Kisenge and Malonga without fight, before continuing for Sandoa, while the 3rd Battalion went straight for Sandoa.

At the time, the FAZ had very few troops deployed along the border: only 76 were stationed in Dilolo, 35 in Kolwezi, 30 in Kapanga, 20 at Sandoa, 18 at Kasaji, and 6 at Kisenge. Other units based in Shaba included the 2nd Airborne Battalion at Lubumbashi, and the 3rd Commando Battalion at Kamina AB – but both were only at 35% of their authorized strength. Furthermore, all the units

One of FAZA's MB.326GB-pilots, as seen with his mount in the early 1970s. Although very proud of themselves and their aircraft, in April 1977 pilots of the 212th Squadron flatly refused to fly combat sorties because of a mere rumour that the insurgents might be equipped with SA-7s. (Pit Weinert Collection)

Kamina. Another battalion (with three companies) was to attack in an eastern direction right from the start, with the intention of securing Kolwezi. Arguably the most daring element of the FNLC's advance was the task of the 4th Battalion, which was to take Kamina, with the nearby air base, a strategic point in this part of Zaire. Once these objectives were in their possession, Mbumba's insurgents expected to have more than 50% of Shaba under their control. This was to enable them to announce the establishment of their own government and spread their ideology within the population.[31]

Led by Gregoire Mulombo and a disproportionate number of high-ranking officers – including General Mufu (one of the

in question lacked heavy weapons and were short on ammunition and other supplies. Foremost, local officers had neglected multiple indications that preceded the invasion: they not only failed to forward related reports to their superiors, but even to put their own troops on alert.[32] Thus, although warned well in advance, the FAZ offered next to no resistance: most of its ground units simply turned around and fled. Indeed, although the FAZA deployed most of the MB.326s of the 212th Squadron from Kamina AB to Kolwezi 'Main' airfield as early as of 8 March 1977, these flew not one combat sortie: pilots of the unit commanded by Lieutenant Tshitunda refused to fly because of faulty intelligence about the insurgents being equipped

Contrary to their Sukisa-flying colleagues, FAZA's transport pilots proved their worth during the I Shaba War, by flying dozens of supply sorties. This pre-delivery photo shows the first of three DHC-5s acquired by the Zairian air force. (Tom Cooper Collection)

with Soviet-made Strela-2 (ASCC/NATO code 'SA-7 Grail') man-portable air defence missiles (MANPADs).

On 9 March, Mobutu – who was presiding over a meeting of his political party in Gadolite, in northern Zaire at the time of the invasion – personally issued an order for a FAZ counter-offensive. Next to nothing happened: the MB.326-unit at Kolwezi 'Main' merely received few loads of fuel, ammunition and spares delivered by one of the C-130Hs of the FAZA and a Boeing 737 airliner requisitioned from Air Zaire. Even once the Deputy Chief of Staff FAZ, Colonel Mampa Ngakwe Salamayi, arrived in Kolwezi to take over as commander of operations, the Zairian military did not move. It was only after Mobutu made a call to Tshitunda to repeat his order for attack, that Sukisa-pilots embarked their aircraft and started flying. However, instead of targeting the insurgents, one of them hit a column of FAZ troops, while another bombed a village inside Zambia.[33]

Meanwhile, the insurgents continued advancing almost at will: on 10 March, they secured Mutshatsha, then brought in reinforcements, by train, from Texeira de Sousa in Angola to Kasaji, and then took Sandoa on 13 March following a short fight with the 3rd Company of the 4th Infantry Battalion FAZ, recently re-deployed from Kinshasa.[34] Sandoa was of particularly symbolic nature because during the final battles of the Katangan Secession War in 1963, it was there that Tshombe-loyalists had made their 'last stand'. Unsurprisingly, the local population proved largely sympathetic to the marching Tigers – at least until these robbed all the banks and then confiscated all the vehicles they could lay their hands upon, which was widely misinterpreted as an expression of their leftist ideology. Furthermore, in the Kisenge area, the FNLC's columns quickly ran into several settlements of Angolan refugees, mostly families of members of the FNLA and some of UNITA. While a risky move, because this was likely to bring the Katangan insurgents into a direct and time-consuming clash with Angolan insurgents, this was certainly no accident: the MPLA, FNLC's primary supporter, was keen to have the Tigers destroy the bases of its enemies inside Zaire.

Kamanyola's Intervention

As the advance of the Tigers went on, Belgian military intelligence scrambled to obtain precise information on their movements. Instead of accepting reports from the FAZ's Chief of Staff, General Bumba Moaso Djogi, who was absent from Kinshasa and actually not in the picture about the situation, but citing an 'invasion of the Shaba by a horde of Cuban-Russian-paid mercenaries' – the Belgians quickly concluded that the sympathetic population was clearly a major factor in favour of the FLNC. Indeed, before long, reports began surfacing about the possibility of anti-government revolts in much of the Bas-Congo and Kasai – both of which were traditionally opposed to Mobutu. Eventually, the Belgians concluded that the main axis of Tigers' advance was the route from Dilolo to Mutshatsha, rather than the 'easier' one, in the direction of Kapanga. This led them to the wrong conclusion that the primary objective of the FNLC was Kolwezi. Advised correspondingly, the FAZ began deploying its units on the eastern side of the crisis zone. The first to arrive in Kolwezi, on 10 March 1977, was the 2nd Airborne Battalion (225 troops). After finding the place still under control of the FAZ, the 1st and the 2nd Companies of this unit – with a total of 93 troops – continued further west, until running into the insurgent vanguard in the Maionga area. The 'elite' unit of the Zairian military was then quickly routed by the insurgents: its troops fled from the battlefield after only a short clash, leaving behind a significant arsenal of arms, including an old 75mm field gun – which was promptly turned against its former owners. Nevertheless, as the FNLC and the FAZ deployed additional troops into the Kolwezi area, a sort of stalemate developed, and next to no fighting was reported for the next two weeks.[35]

Meanwhile, the entire 1st Kamanyola Division was mobilised and ordered to deploy into positions to confront the FNLC. However, the very moment its elements began to move, they found themselves confronted with immense logistical problems: the first two battalions of the 11th Brigade were airlifted to Kolwezi on 12 March. They, and the survivors of the 2nd Airborne Battalion were put under the command of Lieutenant-Colonel Mankoti, and ordered to hold Kasaji until the arrival of reinforcements. However, when this group moved towards their objective, later the same day, it ran into an insurgent ambush and was routed, leaving behind dozens of dead and nearly all of its weapons. Mankoti took two days to re-assemble his surviving troops at Kakopa, a village about 10 kilometres east of Kasaji, and prepare a counterattack. In the meantime, on 15 March, Mobutu dismissed Mankoti's superior

– and commander of the Kamanyola Division – Colonel Mampa Ngakwe Salamay, and appointed Colonel Eluki Monga Andu in his place. Although knowing that his troops were critically short on ammunition, food and water, Andu insisted on a counterattack. Eventually, Mankoti didn't need to move forward: on 18 March his force ambushed an insurgent column, killed 15 and destroyed three Land Rovers, in exchange for losing two of his own troops killed and two taken prisoner. Reporting this clash as the result of a 'counter-attack', the good Lieutenant-Colonel has finally achieved the first 'victory' for the FAZ.[36]

A row of Mirage 5Ms from 211th Squadron. While taken on the tarmac of Kamina AB, and depicting scenes similar to those of April and May 1978, this photograph was probably shot during a joint Franco-Zairian exercise in 1978. (via Pit Weinert)

Loss of Mutshatsha

Enraged by the slow progress and repeated failures of his military, on 19 March Mobutu flew to Kolwezi, but returned to Kinshasa the same evening because of other affairs. Nothing happened for another four days and thus, when the Zairian strongman returned to Kolwezi on 23 March, he completely reorganized the command staff: he appointed Colonel Andu as the Commander of the Operations, with Colonel Sasa Mwaka as Deputy, and ordered them to prepare an elaborate plan for a counteroffensive. Knowing that they were not only lacking troops but especially supplies, Andu and Mwaka did nothing in regards of offensive operations for the next two weeks: instead, they took care to bring in reinforcements and start stocking supplies.[37]

Thus, it was on Major Tshibangu, Commander of the Commando Centre at Kota-Koli, to try stopping further insurgent advances. During the night from 23 to 24 March, Tshibangu loaded a company of his troops on a train for Mutshatsha, where they arrived the next morning. Once there, and lacking any maps of the area, he quickly scouted the battlefield and then positioned his troops around the bridge over the Mukelesha River, about 20 kilometres west of Mutshatsha. On 25 March 1977, at 1345 hours, the insurgents – who were very familiar with the local terrain – easily outmanoeuvred Tshibangu's command. Indeed, they quickly overpowered the small garrison and secured Mutshatsha.

Crisis of the FAZ

Meanwhile, FAZA's C-130Hs were used to haul additional troops, ammunition and food to Kamina AB and to Kolwezi. For unknown reasons, the use of DHC-5 Buffalos – which could carry up to 50 troops – was strictly prohibited by General Bumba Moaso Djogi, commander of Kamina AB. However, Mobutu never took action against this officer who was to cause many problems for most of the involved units in the following days.

On 25 March, the C-130s deployed a company of pygmies from Kitona to Kolwezi. Commanded by Lieutenant-Colonel Mukobo, these then joined survivors of the 2nd Airborne Battalion and two battalions of the 11th Brigade of the Kamanyola Division, and were assigned the task of securing a defence line from Nasandoya to Kayemembe, and linking-up with Major Tshibangu's force. Encouraged by this development, Tshibangu suggested a pincer attack on Mutshatsha. This was launched on 27 March at 1330hrs, with his company attacking from one side, and Lieutenant-Colonel Mukobo's battalion from another – but quickly failed in the face of insurgent resistance. Moreover, at this crucial moment the FAZ troops were failed by the FAZA: the Sukisa-pilots still continued to refuse flying attack sorties and thus did nothing. Only their Mirage-flying colleagues in Kamina attempted to fly combat sorties; however, their aircraft almost instantly began developing problems with their armament: precise details of this remains unclear, but it seems that their guns were frequently jamming, and most of their bombs failed to detonate. Foremost, they tended to launch their sorties at exactly the same time every day, in turn losing the moment of surprise. Eventually, Kinshasa issued a request for assistance, and Paris deployed a mission of armament specialists. One of them, Jean-Paul Bour, recalled:

> I was assigned to Zaire from March 1977 and sent to Kamina to solve these weapons issues. I had 24hr notice to get there and had to stay for a week as there was no aircraft for the return. I had no change of clothes, no toilet bag, and little idea of how or where to feed myself. The latter was solved when I meet three French paratroopers on site. The faulty weapons were fixed and the bombings became more effective.[38]

Unsurprisingly, by 29 March the insurgents had managed to secure even the town of Kapanga, more than 60 kilometres north of Sandoa.

Unavailingly, yet another failure of the FAZ prompted Mobutu into two additional reorganizations of the command staff FAZ. The second of these resulted in the appointment of Brigadier-General Singa Boyenge Mosambay – Chief-of-Staff FAZA – in command of all the forces in Shaba. Upon arriving in Kolwezi on 29 March, Mosambay first ordered his communication officer to requisition AN/PRC-10 radio sets from the headquarters of the local gendarmerie, and distribute these to all the FAZ units deployed in the field, together with a liaison officer. While this proved anything other than sufficient, at least the commander was now in touch with all the headquarters of his subordinated units.

Next, Mosambay gathered all the Sukisa-pilots in the squadron ready room at Kolwezi 'Main' and threatened to strip them of their ranks and replace the entire staff of the unit should they not start flying again. This time at least a few were convinced to fly reconnaissance sorties, for which their aircraft were equipped with underwing pods with three reconnaissance cameras (one pointed forward, one vertical camera, and one pointed to the port side of the aircraft). Their operations finally helped identify primary concentrations of the FNLC.[39]

On 30 March, two airborne battalions commanded by Colonel Songambele arrived in Kolwezi. Mosambay promptly ordered them to establish a new defence line at Kanzenze, about 60 kilometres east of Kolwezi. However, and for unknown reasons, Songambele deployed his unit at Munanga, about 139 kilometres east of Kolwezi, while only positioning his headquarters at Kanzeze. To the luck of the FAZ, the deployment of Songambele's unit was not countered by the FNLC. This was of critical importance because Songambele's force was originally planned to be reinforced by the 845-strong 12th Brigade of the Kamanyola Division. Commanded by Colonel Ikuku Moboto, this unit was based near Kitona AB, on the Atlantic coast, 500 kilometres west of Kinshasa and nearly 1500 kilometres away from the battlefields of southern Shaba: it had to be airlifted to Kamina with the help of DC-8 transports of AirZaire on 8 April. However, on the next morning Colonel Ikuku was arrested on order from General Djogi, officially, 'for unknown reasons'. Eventually, it took an intervention by Mosanbay with Mobutu for Ikuku to be allowed to return to his unit: back in command, he then had to march with his troops for 30 kilometres to the nearest train station, and then requisition a train to Kolwezi, where he arrived more than 36 hours later than originally planned. Once again, Djogi was not even reprimanded for disturbing a major military operation.[40]

The first 500 troops from the 12th Brigade thus arrived in the Kanzenze area only during the night from 9 to 10 April.

Operation *Ververine*

It was at this critical moment in time that – on requests from Kinshasa and Paris, and with US financial backing – Morocco launched its military intervention in Zaire, Operation *Verveine*, on 6 April 1977. In the course of this enterprise, a regiment of about 1,200-1,500 Moroccan Army troops led by General Ahmed Dlimi was deployed with the help of commercial airliners and 13 of AdA's C.160 Transall transports to Zaire. Aswell as the French, the Moroccan deployment was supported by the Egyptian Air Force (EAF), which for this purpose sent several of its Antonov An-12B transports to Zaire.[41]

The Moroccan deployment is worth some attention: it was based on the fact that the Moroccan King Hassan II was not only at odds with the Organisation of African Unity (OAU) because of the situation in Western Sahara (claimed by Morocco), but also – and exactly like Mobutu – he manoeuvred on the international scene with the aim of presenting his country as a 'bulwark against Soviet subversion' in Africa. Correspondingly, Hassan II not only explained his decision with the OAU's support for the anti-Moroccan insurgency in Western Sahara, but also in terms of the FLNC's 'secessionist roots', and the 'Soviet threat'. With hindsight, such statements cannot but be commented upon with some irony: after all, one of the FNLC's regulars captured in the Kolwezi area clearly stated, 'First we were trained by the Portuguese and after that by the Cubans – but there are no Cubans (supporting the FNLC) now'.[42]

Eventually, it was only once the Moroccan officers arrived at Kolwezi, together with the first group of 200 of their troops, that the

An injured Zairian soldier is evacuated from one of FAZA's SA.330 Pumas (registration 9T-HP1) that returned from the battlefield. Helicopters of the Zairian air force played an important role in supporting the advance on Mutshatsha and the subsequently pursuit of the FNLC. (Pit Weinert Collection)

A C-130H Hercules transport of the Royal Moroccan Air Force unloading M113 armoured personnel carrier of the Moroccan army at Kolwezi 'Main' airport. (Albert Grandolini Collection)

FAZ officers managed to finalize their plan for a counteroffensive. According to the same, they established two major task forces:

- Ikuku Front, including the 12th Brigade of the Kamanyola Division, which was to attack along the border to Zambia in a western direction to Mutshatsha; and
- Mukobo Front, including the 11th Brigade of the Kamanyola Division, an infantry battalion of the FAZ commanded by Major Shabani, another infantry battalion of the FAZ commanded by Major Ngoie, and one company of the FAZ commanded by Lieutenant Misela, which was to attack from Kamina towards the south, with the objective of Sandoa, and then on to Dilolo.

The crew of an AML-60 armoured car from Colonel Ikuku's unit that defeated the insurgents on the Lufupa train station taking rest outside their vehicle. Note the mix of camouflage jackets with Leopard pattern trousers, as issued to troops serving with the 1st Kamanyola Division. (Albert Grandolini Collection)

Attack of the Railroad Snake

During the next two days, the FAZ was foremost busy preparing its offensive. Correspondingly, General Kikunda Ombala – the Chief of Staff of the 2nd Group FAZA – arrived in Kolwezi, to 'talk' with pilots of the 212th Squadron. Precise details about what happened next remain unknown but, eventually – and rather 'suddenly' – all the Sukisa-fliers proved 'highly enthusiastic' about fighting the FNLC. On 12 April, as the next Moroccan contingent of 420 troops arrived at Kolwezi 'Main', they rocketed insurgent positions in Lubudi and the train station at Kayembei. Later during the day, the 1st Company, 122nd Battalion of the 12th Brigade of the Kamanyola Division ran into an ambush while approaching the train station in Lufupa: without even trying to return fire, the unit fell apart and fled. Its commander, Captain Kamba, was found 20 kilometres further to the rear: he was dismissed and replaced by 2nd Lieutenant Bumba. During the following night, the infantry battalion led by Major Shabani experienced its first action, too: while marching in the direction of Nasandoye, it ran into an insurgent unit wearing FAZ uniforms. By the time the troops recognized whom are they facing it was too late: nine were killed and 21 injured. According to officials in Kinshasa, the FNLC lost only seven.[43]

On the morning of 13 April, the Sukisas rocketed the towns of Matanda and Sakalezi, while Mirages bombed the Mutshatsha area. Whilst reportedly having 'good psychological impact' upon the FNLC, the air strikes failed to prevent the insurgents from attempting to set up another ambush at the Lufupa train station. However, while launching an attempt to take this position, Colonel Ikuku sent a squadron of his AML armoured cars forward: taken by surprise, the insurgents quickly lost their commander – Lieutenant Tshimwanga Moise – and fled from the battlefield. After this defeat, the FNLC nick-named Ikuku the 'Railroad Snake' (*'serpent des railes'*) – and some of the FAZ troops involved were more than happy to apply corresponding inscriptions on their vehicles.

The Moroccan Blitz

The availability of additional Moroccan troops enabled the Zairian and Moroccan commanders to reinforce the Ikuku Front through the addition of the battalion commanded by Major el-Madany Abdel-Qalik. This unit moved out of Kolwezi on 15 April 1977, but 15 kilometres outside of the town had a traffic accident in which the driver of commander's jeep was killed. This was the first Moroccan soldier killed in this campaign. Nevertheless, the unit continued its march and joined Colonel Ikuku's 12th Brigade at Lufupa on 16 April. It was followed by a Moroccan artillery unit, which joined the 122nd Battalion FAZ for an attack on the bridge over the Lufupa River, five kilometres outside the town, on 16 April. This operation was highly successful, and concluded without any loses.

Moroccan troops atop one of their M113s during the advance on Mutshatsha. Note that the 'sand overall' livery of all the Moroccan vehicles deployed in Zaire during the Operation *Ververine*. (Albert Grandolini Collection)

As additional Moroccan units joined the FAZ troops, a subsequent advance came forward at an increasing pace. On 21 April, combined Zairian and Moroccan units secured the towns of Sakalezi and Kayembe. Three days later, the FAZ and its allies were already on

A FAZ jeep with recoilless gun calibre 106mm and Moroccan troops in the Mutshatsha area, on 26 April 1977. (Albert Grandolini Collection)

Column of Moroccan Army's UNIMOG trucks on advance towards the Angolan border, in early May 1977. (Albert Grandolini Collection)

the outskirts of Mutshatsha. The attack on this town began with a series of air strikes, followed by an artillery barrage and then a pincer attack of the 11th Brigade, supported by AMLs, on the morning of 25 April. The FNLC did not offer any resistance: following its trashing at Lufupa train station, it started a hurried withdrawal. On the next day, Mobutu was thus free to stage a theatrical 'inspection of the frontlines': flying a C-130H escorted by four MB.326s, he arrived in Kolwezi for an 'on-the-spot assessment of developments.' On the tarmac, teenage girls danced to welcome him, punctuating their gyrations with cries of, 'Our guide, our faith!' Together with him arrived a large group of foreign journalists to whom Mobutu announced that, 'Zaire will do everything to crush Soviet influence in Africa'.[44]

Luke-warm Pursuit

The defeat at Lufupa and the quick loss of Mutshatsha left the entire FNLC in a state of shock. Overconfident after easily defeating the FAZ at earlier opportunities, the insurgents not only proved unable to hold their lines, but refused to do so: they fled, leaving behind their dead and wounded, and significant quantities of arms and ammunition. After receiving corresponding intelligence, the FAZ put all the available units under the command of Colonel Ikuku and ordered him to launch a pursuit. The resulting advance – which became known as the 'Moroccan Blitz' amongst the locals – was supported by FAZA's Alouette and Puma helicopters (some of these flown by Moroccan pilots), which greatly eased the task of tracking insurgent movements, and sometimes guided air strikes on these, too. The Sukisa-pilots of the 212th Squadron flew additional attacks, but on 29 April the aircraft flown by Lieutenants Siamune and Bokolo hit the command post of the FAZ in Masoji by mistake. Bokolo was quickly declared guilty and severely punished.[45]

The Moroccans reached Sanikosa by 4 May, while the FAZ then secured Musaji, on 7 May, without encountering any resistance. The pilot of a Puma helicopter carrying Colonel Ikuku Moboto, and several of his aides, lost his direction the following night, and was forced to land in the bush, but the group was found on the following morning and the successful commander returned to

Troops of the Kamanyola Division taking a break during the pursuit of the retreating FNLC, in late May 1977. (FNLC release)

Musaji – only to order his unit to continue the advance. Further increasing the pressure, Mirage 5Ms of the 211th Squadron repeatedly hit Dilolo. Kasaji, Sandoa and Kisenge: while remaining 'not particularly effective' in terms of scoring hits, they left lasting impressions upon the FNLC. Indeed, there are clear indications that almost everything flying was claimed to be a 'Mirage', and reports that some of their strafing runs – sometimes directed by Mobutu himself, who was present at Kamina AB and wore the uniform of a Lieutenant-General FAZ – caused outright panic within insurgent ranks.

Kasaji was retaken on the morning of 12 May, though not without problems caused by an increasing number of mines left behind by the insurgents. Mines represented the primary threat during the following days too, as the combined Zairian-Moroccan forces continued their advance: Djongo was retaken by two FAZ battalions on 18 May, and the bridge on the Divuma River during the following

Moroccan troops waiting to board French C.160 Transall transports for their deployment against the FNLC, in the Katanga/Shaba Province of Zaire, in April 1977. (Albert Grandolini Collection)

FAZ troops, together with one of the Moroccan officers (background, with beret), during the Shaba I campaign. (US DoD)

night. The FNLC blew up three other bridges on the Luashi River, south of Kisenge, but Major Tshiembe and his battalion took Luashi on the morning of 19 May, while Major Tshibangu and his unit secured Kisenge the same afternoon.

The next day, General Mosambay joined Colonel Ikuku Moboto: the two officers then led two platoons of FAZ infantry, followed by two squadrons of Moroccans, into Dilolo: the town was captured without fighting by 2230hrs the same night. The last FNLC insurgents left Zaire on board a train including 15 cars, and carrying six AMLs, three tractors, two Unimog trucks, and one Land Rover, plus all the money seized from banks and private enterprises over the last 80 days.

Four days later, a triumphant Mobutu announced the defeat of the FNLC. On the contrary, although meanwhile clocking up to 240 sorties in total (including those against their own troops and 'targets' in Zambia), the 212th Squadron remained unlucky: on 24 May 1977, Lieutenant Nyembo Pauni crashed on landing in Kolwezi, killing himself and Lieutenant Bokolo.[46]

Overall, the FAZ suffered about 219 casualties (including 30 fatalities) during the I Shaba War; the Moroccans lost eight killed in action, while the losses of the FNLC remain unknown.[47]

A pair of FAZ's AMLs: notable in the rear is an AML-90 with the inscription 'Serpent de Rail', applied following successful Zairian attack on the Lufupa train station. (Albert Grandolini Collection)

Spring Cleaning

Despite serious concerns of the Belgian and French military intelligence services that the insurgents might 'disappear' and 'melt' into the local population, and Zairian concerns that the FNLC might attempt to 'infiltrate' the Kamina AB, nothing similar happened – at least not immediately. The reason was that the FAZ subsequently launched a campaign that can only be described as an 'act of collective punishment': its troops raided all over south-western Shaba, but especially the Manika District of Kolwezi, detaining and murdering thousands of 'suspected collaborators' and 'traitors'. The Lumbas were targeted in particular: over 70,000 people from this ethnic group felt forced to flee to Angola by the end of 1977.[48] This was something with which neither Brussels nor Paris were in agreement: while Mobutu was insisting in public that the entire affair was an Angolan-Cuban-Soviet conspiracy with the intention of spreading Communism into Zaire, his troops clearly

FAZA's Sukisas returned to the combat only towards the end of Shaba I. This view of a pair demonstrates their usual weapon configuration during this conflict: pods with 7.62mm machine guns on inboard underwing pylons, drop tanks, and Matra F2 pods for unguided 68mm rockets. (Pit Weinert Collection)

acted according to sectarian motives. The Belgians and the French correctly concluded that – irrespective of the leftist ideology of the FNLC – the actual aim of the insurgency was to establish an independent Katanga. It is thus almost unnecessary to point out that the mistreatment, atrocities and massacres of the Lumbas by the FAZ during the second half of 1977 greatly contributed to the quick recovery of the FNLC: many of the refugees were to return to Zaire – well armed – less than a year later.

Next, Mobutu turned against his own military. First, he secured the deployment of a sizeable team of pilots and ground personnel from the EAF in support of the Mirage-equipped 211th Squadron. This is how it happened that pilots Reda Meshref, Mohammed Makarem, Medhat Labib and about 40 technicians, all led by Colonel Mohammed Weziry Makarem, arrived at Kamina AB, about a week after the end of combat operations. Precise details about this deployment remain scarce, it is only known that the Egyptians did try to train additional Zairian pilots and ground personnel on Mirages for two months, 'despite' tropical weather, before being withdrawn: they never flew any kind of combat operations for the FAZA.[49]

Meanwhile, and despite the apparent success of the FAZ in what subsequently became known either as 'Shaba I' or the 'I Shaba War', during the Spring of 1978 Mobutu purged most of his existing units. Part of the reason was a little-known mutiny of some officers and NCOs in the Kivus, who were still sympathising with whatever was left of the Lumumbist and Simba movements of the 1960s; another part was related to little other than inter-service intrigues by such officers as General Djogi. Furthermore, while supposedly aiming to sort out incompetent officers, Mobutu severely punished anybody considered 'not exactly loyal' to him and the clique of his closest aides: 19 different officers were court-martialled and sentenced to death, while 70 high-ranking civil servants either lost their jobs or were incarcerated for years. Eventually, contrary to the planned expansion of the military, the purge resulted in a significant decline in the total manpower of the FAZ: the ground forces alone lost nearly 25% of their officers and other ranks. Unsurprisingly, Kinshasa was forced to contract Belgian and French advisors to start training multiple new units. Finally, Mobutu made another mistake when reaching the decision to reinforce his support for the armed Angolan opposition, especially UNITA, but also for separatists in the Cabinda enclave. In this fashion, he not only diverted additional valuable resources from his own military, but also breached existing treaties with the government in Luanda, in turn causing the Angolan government to unleash the FNLC again.

CHAPTER 6
II SHABA WAR

While the Zairian military managed to successfully conclude the I Shaba War with relatively limited help from Morocco and elsewhere abroad, nothing similar can be said for the II Shaba War, which erupted only a year later. On the contrary, during the latter conflict it was France that played the decisive role. Indeed, the determining moment of that affair was the firm stance of the government in Paris (and the French military). To some, this was surprising because Congo was never a French colony, nor any kind of a dependent territory in the past. However, a closer look at related affairs reveals a slightly different picture. Paris not only considered Kinshasa a 'bastion of resistance against growing Soviet influence in Africa' – which, to many in the West appeared to be spreading like a wild fire – but also insisted on becoming involved in what was certainly the second largest Francophone nation of the World: an aspect of crucial importance for the self-imposed image of 'Mother France'.

Ironically, it remains next to unknown in public that the French were maintaining ties to the Katangans since the last year of the original Secession War: as of 1962, French officers began replacing

Mbumba (third from the left, with glasses) seen while planning with his commanders, in May 1978. The leader of the FNLC did not enter Zaire during the II Shaba War: he remained inside Angola while communicating with his commanders only via radio. (FNLC release)

the Belgians that – following the installation of a 'moderate' central government in Kinshasa – dropped Tshombe like a hot rock. Indeed, at a certain point during that year, strategists in Paris may even have developed a plan for helping establish Katanga as an independent country, yet also one that would join the Francophone community on the African continent. A similar sentiment was clearly visible for years afterwards. For example, according to a report by the French ambassador to Zaire, Andre Ross, for the Franco-American summit of April 1978, Shaba should have been treated as a, 'de-facto occupied territory and by no means integral part of Zaire'. Concluding the above stance, Ross estimated the probability of secession with outside help as 'very likely in near future'. All these factors were based on the very accurate information acquired by diverse French intelligence services, all of which were well-positioned in the region. As it turned out, later on, the Belgians had had even more precise details in this regard.[50]

Keeping all this in mind, and combining such facts with the atrocities of the FAZ against the Lumbas in 1977, it is little surprising that the next crisis in the Shaba was not only 'unavoidable', but indeed: to follow within only a few months.

Recovery of the FNLC

Shaba I should have served as a warning to Mobutu, but especially to his intelligence services. Nothing similar was the case. Indeed: the Zairian military and civilian intelligence agencies had once again managed to ignore a number of warnings: one intelligence officer that warned about the coming invasion was declared a 'panic-maker' for filling his report, and was punished. On the contrary, thanks to the massive influx of refugees to Angola, the FNLC was quick to rebuild its strength. In a matter of a few months, the movement had about 7,000 personnel under arms. Replenished from extensive stocks of the MPLA/FAPLA, these were organized into a dozen battalions. At least as important was the fact that the Katangese Gendarmes managed to organize a conspiracy and 'sleeper cells' including between 300 and 500 activists in the Kolwezi area (especially in the Manika District), which were to be activated at the start of the next invasion attempt. The activists in question had also provided excellent intelligence on the FAZ's positions, activities and weaknesses, while in turn the Zairian authorities were entirely unaware of their presence.[51]

The new operation – which resulted in what became known as the II Shaba War – was much better planned. It not only came from Angola again, but included an 'outflanking' manoeuvre via the poorly protected Lunda territory of Zambia, and emphasised multiple quick advances on the Kolwezi airport and the Kamina AB, with the intention of denying these crucial installations to the FAZ and the FAZA. On the negative side, in order to better avoid the effects of the FAZA's air strikes and Zairian artillery, this time the invading force was infiltrated into its starting positions in small groups over a period of 45 days, and also split into no less than six battalions – total of between 3,000 and 4,000 troops.[52]

The FNLC forces advanced in two main groups: one from Angola on Mutshatsha and the other from Zambia on Kolwezi. After crossing Zambia, the first two columns of the eastern group entered Zaire in the first minutes of 11 May 1978. Encountering no resistance on the border, they reached Kolwezi two days later. Like a year before, the FAZ actually received a warning about an incoming attack, and thus most of the 212th Squadron FAZA was forward deployed at Kolwezi 'Main'. However, the 14th Brigade of the 1st Kamanyola Division did nothing before the insurgents reached the town. Furthermore, because this civilian facility lacked suitable accommodations, all the Sukisa-pilots, as well as those flying diverse helicopters, were staying in a nearby villa. Early on the morning of 13 May 1978, they were all awakened by sounds of uninterrupted fire: indeed, the home in which the pilots slept was one of the principal objectives of the FNLC's attacks. Fortunately for the FAZA, the insurgents were held up by several AML-90s. However, in turn, nobody could leave the villa and go to man the aircraft at the airport, south of the town.

At 1000hrs in the morning, FAZA's pilots received a radio message from a civilian pilot who attempted to land at Kolwezi and came under intensive ground fire and was forced into a rapid climb. With this news, it became clear that the insurgents had overrun Kolwezi 'Main'. As the subsequent developments were to show, they had destroyed four or five, and badly damaged two, MB.326GBs, and also burned six Cessna 310s, and at least one SA.330 Puma and SA.318 Alouette III each. With this, the entire 212th Squadron was knocked out of the fight right at the start of this campaign.[53]

At 1630hrs, a sole Mirage 5 overflew Kolwezi without intervening. The local FAZ troops needed no further orders: all quickly withdrew outside the town, followed by surviving FAZA personnel: the latter reached Kamina AB only four days later. At the main military base of Kolwezi, the FNLC thus managed to seize a number of intact military vehicles, including at least four AML-60s, two AML-90s, and three Panhard M3 APCs. While all were supposed to be in

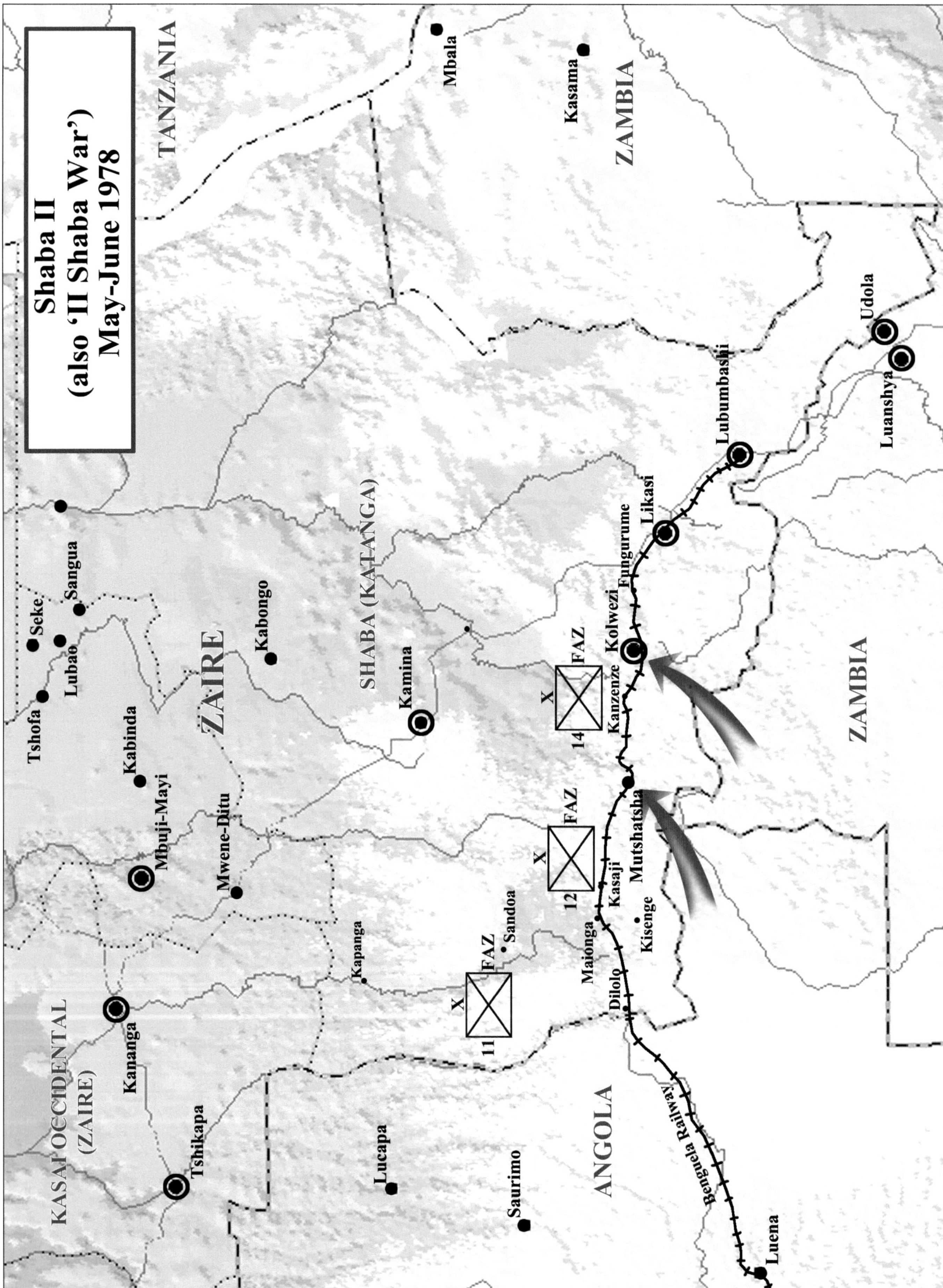

Map of the FNLC's routes of advance into the Shaba province, in May 1978, with the dispositions of three of FAZ's major brigades deployed in the area. (Map by Tom Cooper)

Wreckage of two out of at least five of FAZA's MB.326GBs destroyed by the FNLC at Kolwezi 'Main' on the morning of 13 May 1978. (photos by Marc Steegmans)

Of note in this photograph of the same wreckage are the machinegun pods on inboard underwing stations. (photo by Marc Steegmans)

unserviceable condition, and thus presumed as 'beyond the reach of insurgent capability to repair them', at least the three AMLs were quickly brought into action. In the meantime, other FNLC units had secured Mutshatsha and a number of other, minor towns. Once again, much of Shaba was under the insurgent control.

Western Reaction

Initially upon taking Kolwezi, the FNLC insurgents had behaved in a friendly fashion to the locals. They proved well-disciplined, eager to portray themselves as a 'liberation army', and concentrated upon delivering a political message to the ethnic Lundas – who in turn proved eager to reveal any FAZ troops that attempted to hide. About 2,500 white expatriates – including employees of the GECAMINES and their families – were not molested: on the contrary, the management of their company even issued a memorandum stating, 'FNLC: Positive Approach to the Local Population regardless of the Colour of their Skin'. Indeed, early on, the insurgents went as far as to spare any captured FAZ troops that proved willing to join them: however, any soldiers that refused to join were quickly liquidated.[54]

Then the situation began to worsen: an American civilian was accused of being a mercenary, and shot to death, while seven members of the French military mission attached to the FAZ went missing – and were later found dead, killed by the FNLC. Also missing was a group of Moroccan advisors: like their French colleagues, these were executed following an order of the 'Revolutionary Court' set up for such cases. Finally, a light aircraft attempting to land at Kolwezi airport was fired upon: its Belgian pilot managed to accelerate in time and return to Lubumbashi, where he confirmed the rumours about the takeover of Kolwezi by an 'unidentified force'. Unknown to them, the expatriate workers and their families were soon in grave danger: the FNLC eventually took over 2,000 foreigners as hostages, including 28 Americans.[55]

This was already obvious to all those on the end of a 'hotline' established between government agencies in Belgium, France and the USA with the intention of securing lives of their citizens in Zaire. Thus, it remains unclear whether the earlier memorandum by the management of the GECAMINES was a misjudgement or a conscious attempt to avoid panic amongst – foremost Belgian – expatriates. However, Brussels, Paris and Washington could not find an agreement about how to react: the Belgians and the French could not agree about anything, while the Americans then decided to go their own way. The US company Morris-Knudsen, heavily present in the Shaba, and in possession of several of their own aircraft deployed in Zaire, thus became the first to issue a warning about a possible evacuation to all of its employees.

What is certain is that that the chief of the French Military Mission to Zaire (MMF), Colonel Yves Grass, was already urging Mobutu to deploy the FAZ into a counterattack on Kolwezi. Almost as overconfident of the capabilities of the Zairian military, and its mobility and fire-power in particular, as Mobutu, Grass was rather surprised by the lack of reaction: only his repeated calls and a FNLC attack on Mutshatsha had finally made Mobutu aware of the scale of the new invasion. Even then, he only mobilised the 133rd Infantry Battalion and the 311th Airborne Battalion of the FAZ.

Suicide Squad

To be fair to him, Mobutu was not amused at being shoved around by ex-colonial powers, deciding what to do on his soil behind his back. At the end of the day he was a ruler in Kolwezi as well – at least as far as the map of his country was showing it. Boosted by the false dawn of the previous year's victory over FNLC, Mobutu issued the order for the 311th Battalion FAZ to prepare its own military intervention, independently from the allies.

On 14 May 1978, it became known that nine Belgian and one Italian employee of the GECAMINES had been killed in Kolwezi. This was the decisive moment for the French: losing patience with the Belgians, who were still unwilling to take any decisive action, Paris decided to go its own way. From now on there were two

Some of the armoured vehicles left behind by the FAZ in Kolwezi, including (from front towards the rear), two AML-60s, and a pair of M3 light armoured personnel carriers. Note the inscription 'Serpent de Rail' on the vehicle in the foreground. (Albert Grandolini Collection)

military operations in preparation. The French and Belgians had also set different objectives: Paris wanted not only to save the lives of its citizens but also to destroy the FNLC as a fighting force. On the contrary, overcautious due to its earlier experiences in the Congo – and particularly the Stanleyville campaign of 1964, when the Simbas murdered many of white hostages before the paras could ever reach them – Brussels concentrated on the humanitarian mission to evacuate all Belgians – without any kind of contact with the FNLC, if that was possible of course. Correspondingly, the Belgian soldiers involved were ordered to return fire only in self-defence if attacked. What is of further interest is that the French government only planned to repatriate 'volunteers': anybody who wished to do so could remain in Zaire. This was to be specifically valid for all of the highly qualified mining cadre. Although still reluctant, the Belgians then responded by demanding an unconditional evacuation of all the expatriates from the Kolwezi area, with no exceptions.

Grass was not consulted on any of this, and was desperately trying to get two French army companies from bases in West Africa, to reinforce the FAZ units preparing to land in Kolwezi. Despite many obstacles, the commanding officer of the 311th Battalion – Major Donat Lieko Mahele – managed to prepare the 2nd Company to be dropped over Kolwezi airport from FAZA's C-130Hs. The rest of the battalion was to follow by land. Being one of few competent officers to climb up the career ladder, Mahele knew all the way that this mission had little if any chance to succeed, bearing in mind the rather symbolic strength of the involved company of Zairian Paras. The same was the case with the commander of the company in question: Captain Mosala-Mondja was a graduate of the US Army Command and Staff College.[56]

While the paratroopers were still preparing, Captain M'Bo flew armed reconnaissance with a Mirage 5M. Underway at relatively low altitude, he spotted a convoy of enemy vehicles. Jean-Paul Bour recalled what happened next:

> M'Bo did not shoot, because we intercepted an insurgent radio message that stated that six French members of the *Assistance Militaire Technique* (France's Military Technical Mission in Zaire) had been kidnapped in Kolwezi when the city was taken and were aboard the vehicles. In fact, they had been executed some time before.

At 0500hrs on 16 May 1978, the 2nd Company 311th Para Battalion boarded two C-130Hs at Kamina AB. There are varying reports about the time when the two aircraft reached the drop zone, with sources citing times between 0515hrs and 0630hrs: commanded by resolute Captain Mosala-Monja, the paras then jumped over Kolwezi 'Main'. As the troops came down, they were annihilated, taking 60% casualties to fierce defensive fire of the FNLC. In many respects, those killed before they even hit the ground were the fortunate ones. At 0900, the same aircraft came back to repeat the performance. The results were equally disastrous: of the 120 paras from the 2nd Company, about two dozen were dead and up to 80 others wounded or missing. Nevertheless, Captain Mosala-Monja and survivors fought through to the surrounded headquarters of the 14th Brigade FAZ, a building located about five kilometres from Kolwezi 'Main'.[57]

FNLC Looses the Plot

Meanwhile, a major tragedy was developing at Kolwezi 'Main'. When seeing the destruction of the 2nd Company 311th Para Battalion, Colonel Bosange and about 20 troops from the 14th Brigade FAZ that were still holding out inside the airport buildings – broke and ran, leaving behind 42 defenceless expatriates that gathered there on advice of the FAZ officers with the promise that they would be evacuated by helicopters. The insurgents shot two while approaching the building, then herded everybody inside and opened fire again: 39 were killed in cold blood, one survived badly injured, while two expatriates managed to escape by using a trap door in the toilet and then hiding for four days.

This was probably the most controversial episode of the entire II Shaba War. Usually, full responsibility for this massacre is put upon the FNLC. More recently a new theory surfaced, blaming the FAZ paras for this atrocity: correspondingly, the Zairians killed the Europeans in hope of escalating the conflict and provoking the French retribution and, indeed, destruction of the insurgency. However, the three survivors have put all the blame upon the insurgents.[58]

Elsewhere in Kolwezi, the insurgents and their sympathisers began collecting additional expatriates. Some were shot on the spot. Many others had more luck: a European named Faverjon was arrested by the insurgents and accused of being a Mirage pilot. He managed to avoid execution after a bizarre rant between two of FNLC's NCO's guarding him, after which one of the troops in question told him to 'disappear'.

While many such dramas were developing in Kolwezi, in Kinshasa the French Ambassador Ross and Colonel Grass had forcibly entered Mobutu's residence. Once there, they demanded answers – only to be calmed by the strongman who expressed his confidence that, the situation in Kolwezi was under control. Actually, expecting to receive a report about the outcome of the para-drop by the 311th Battalion, Mobutu was expressing his wishful thinking. Obviously, following the rout of the 2nd Company, no such news ever arrived. Even then, Mobutu continued insisting on his illusions and then descended into praising the excellent training of his elite troops: it remains unknown if he ever knew about the extent of the disaster that befell the unfortunate unit.

Right after the meeting with the Zairian president, Grass went to meet the Chief of Staff FAZ, General Babia. Knowing that the FAZ still had the entire 133rd and 311th Battalions at their disposal, he was still confident – and thus rather shocked when Babia informed him that the assault on the airport failed, while Mahele's column hadn't reached Kolwezi. Although the Zairian continued by repeating Mobutu's day-dreams about the FAZ being 'in full control over the Kolwezi crisis', Colonel Grass slowly began to realise the seriousness of the situation.

Indeed, around the same time FAZ was also feeding similar lies to representatives of multiple foreign companies. Fooled by fake reports and pleased to hear about the supposed success of the FAZ's counter-offensive, manager of Morrison-Knudsen cancelled an evacuation of his employees. On the contrary, the US Army did not take any of the Zairian claims for granted, and the Pentagon thus put the 2nd Brigade of the 82nd Airborne Division on alert, 'just in case'. Also alerted, but not deployed, was the 3rd Battalion, the Queen's Regiment of the British Army. Eventually, US President Jimmy Carter cancelled the intervention of the US military only when Morris-Knudsen managed to evacuate 77 Americans, with the help of helicopters and trucks, from Kolwezi to Musonie, and from there by DC-3s to Kananga.[59]

Mahele's Advance

Unaware of developments in Kolwezi, Major Mahele and the remainder of the 311th Airborne Battalion – including about 200

Troops from Mahele's 311th Airborne Battalion posing with their camouflage uniforms and US-made M16s, outside Kolwezi 'Main' airport. Unsurprisingly, given their rather ill-disciplined behaviour, the Belgians preferred to ignore Zairian reports according to which this vital installation was secured by the FAZ. (Albert Grandolini Collection)

During the II Shaba War, the Mirage 5Ms were piloted mainly by the French. Shortly before the conflict broke out, Georges Bouge was replaced by Jean-Pierre Fartek in the role of instructor. We thus had two French and two or three Zairian pilots. We moved operations to Kamina, about 200 kilometres (125 miles) north-west of Kolwezi. The first Mirage missions were undertaken by one Zairian and two French pilots.

Early on the morning of 17 May, the column of the 311th Airborne Battalion made first contact with the FNLC, about five kilometres west of the Lualaba Bridge. Led by Mahele, the paras attacked, forcing the insurgents to withdraw. They continued the advance until running into an ambush at the Kanzembe train station, only eight kilometres from Kolwezi, but punched through this too. Indeed, around 1100hrs, they reached Kolwezi 'Main', a few kilometres outside the town: Mahele's unit lost six killed and ten wounded during this advance, but managed to secure the crucial installation by 1415hrs. With this, two relatively small FAZ forces were in control of two critical parts of Kolwezi: however, the town itself remained under the control of the insurgents.[60]

Mobutu (left) conferring with Major Mahele (commander of the 311th Battalion and crucial FAZ officer during Shaba II), in front of one of FAZA's C-130Hs. (Mark Lepko Collection)

troops from the 1st Company and the HQ Section – progressed from Lubumbashi mounted on trucks and at their best speed. Their first stop was at the Lualaba Bridge, about 20 kilometres east of Kolwezi. Due to Mobutu's failure to communicate with the French, the unit went in alone – and was then further weakened when the 3rd Company was detached and ordered to remain in Lubumbashi, as a reserve. In turn, the column received at least some sort of air support – in the form of a single Mirage 5M that attacked the Impala Hotel in Kolwezi, used as the HQ of the FNLC – though without causing any damage. In the course of a short conference with the commander of the 133rd Battalion, Mahele decided to use the infantry to reinforce his unit for the further advance on Kolwezi. A pair of Mirages then appeared in the sky with intention of attacking other targets in front of the paras, as recalled by Bour:

French Planning

Meanwhile, top commanders of the French military began planning of an intervention in Kolwezi. Correspondingly, on 17 May 1978, the General Staff of the French Army informed the HQ of the 11th Parachute Division about a possible military intervention in Zaire. When the HQ of the 11th Parachute Division responded with a report that the 2e REP was selected for the task, the General Staff ordered it to be ready for the start of the mission within six hours from the moment an order would be issued.

The HQ of the 11th Parachute Division immediately transmitted this order to the HQ of the 2e REP in Calvi, on Corsica, while separate communication links were established with Paris to sort out a longer list of logistics-related issues, discuss the composition of the involved units, and the necessary transport capabilities.

This was the moment when frequent and intensive exercises had proved their value beyond any doubt, then the staff of the 2e REP proved not only highly professional, but also in a perfect position to fulfil all the orders it received, no matter how 'exceptional' some of these were. In cooperation with the General Staff, the HQ 2e REP first sought a solution for getting the unit all the way to Zaire: after all, Calvi is over 6,000 kilometres away from Kolwezi. Correspondingly, a decision was taken to embark all the troops on board seven Douglas DC-8s – four of these owned by the French air force's Military Transport Command (*Commandement du transport aérien militaire*, COTAM), and three by the UTA – and one Boeing

707 of Air France, for a 10-hours flight to Kinshasa.

Next, the staff of the 2e REP began planning an aerial assault on Kolwezi. In this regard, the French decided to give the crucial role to the C-130s of the FAZA: their calculations had shown that, if the AdA would add two of its C.160 Transalls, there would be enough space on board of all the involved aircraft for about 400 paratroopers – or two complete companies. The aircraft would launch from N'Djili, drop the first wave on Kolwezi 'Small', then return to pick up the remaining troops. The first wave was to secure the airport and link-up with FAZ paras still fighting there. The second was then to secure the centre of the town.

A jump over the Kolwezi 'Main' airport was out of question right from the start, because this was more than five kilometres outside the town, which meant the troops would subsequently have to fight their way to the hostages. Instead, the French expected their paras to jump 'straight into a war zone', and land 'right on the backs' of the insurgents: correspondingly, they intended not to give the enemy any opportunity for organized resistance – except in the Manika District, which was the hotbed of FNLC supporters, and was expected to act as their 'final stronghold', too.

Once on the ground, key points for the 2e REP's attack would be the Old Town and Hotel Impala, GECAMINES' hospital, and the post office. In the New Town, it was to attack the main bridge over the railway line, the Market District and the Main Petrol Station. Furthermore, the 1st Company was to secure the John XXIII High School in southern Kolwezi, and then advance on the Saint Mary Institute. The John XXIII High School had a large flat roof, which presented an excellent observation point, suitable for controlling events around the town, and thus was to act as a headquarters for Erulin and his staff. The 3rd Company was to jump straight into the Old Town, west of the 1st Company, and then clear the terrain in preparation for an assault on the New Town. After securing the GECAMINES Hospital, the 2nd Company was to secure the hostages there and then bring them back to Kolwezi 'Main' for evacuation. The mortar platoon was to be inserted in between the 1st and 2nd Companies, while the small team of engineers received the order to secure the garage of the GECAMINES, adjacent to the hospital, and make use of all the vehicles they could find there. The 4th Company was to act as a reserve and jump in the second wave on a location that would depend upon the situation on the ground. Overall the Legionaries expected to quickly seize control over all the major communications and block potential routes of escape for the FNLC, while exercising pressure upon the insurgents and forcing them to fight for their lives.

An item of bad news for French planners was that they could not expect to receive any kind of close air support (CAS) from the FAZA: Zairian commanders had meanwhile informed Colonel Grass that after 'intensive operations' of the last few days, all the MB.326s and Mirages were grounded for lack of gun ammunition and unguided rockets. Supposedly, so the Zairians said, these were spent in vain by Moroccan pilots in their 'cowboy raids' over Kolwezi, the year before, and there was no time to resupply Kamina AB from stocks in the AdA's depot at N'Djamena International.

Shocks in Kinshasa

This was neither the first nor the last bizarre moment in this affair. In Kinshasa that evening, Colonel Grass met generals Babia and Ginga of the FAZ, the Chief of the US Military Mission to Zaire, Colonel John P Geraci, and his Belgian equivalent, Colonel Bleus, to agree all the final details. Initially, their meeting was run in an atmosphere of good cooperation – until the Belgian refused to do anything else but to evacuate the expatriates. Facing the prospect of losing control over the crucial mining complexes and services of the European cadre of the GECAMINES, the two Zairians panicked. However, adamant to 'restore the order', Grass insisted on nothing less than the French troops searching for and destroying the FNLC in the Kolwezi area. Following a heated exchange, the French simply concluded that Bleus lacked the credibility to take part in the decision-making process. Thus, the Franco-Belgian intervention in the II Shaba War took place as a sort of a paradox: while both operations had similar objectives, the lack of good will for cooperation and an almost childish 'rush for glory' threatened to result in a total chaos on the ground.

This is not to say that Mobutu did not attempt to increase chaos and disagreement through his own actions. Intending to show off – preferably accompanied with 'his heroic troops' – during the evening of 17 May, he announced to the media his intention to pay a visit to the FAZ paratroopers that were still besieged at Kolwezi 'Main'. To say that this raised a few eyebrows would be an understatement: it caused a flurry of telephone calls, telefaxes and face-to-face meetings between – and in – Paris, Brussels, Washington and Kinshasa, with the result of Colonel Erulin receiving an order to prepare his unit for an operation starting on 19 May, a day earlier than originally planned.

When receiving the message, Erulin was on board an airliner underway from Corsica to Zaire. What was going through the mind of already stressed officer in that crucial moment will forever remain a mystery, but one can easily imagine a plethora of swearing so associated with Foreign Legion soldiers directly expressing their feelings.

Too Many Cooks spoil the Broth

While all the paras of the 2e REP were ready and on 'stand by' as of 2000hrs of 17 May, Paris could still not agree with the Belgians about the details of the operation. Nevertheless, Colonel Grass had meanwhile received a dependable report about the situation at the Kolwezi 'Main' – and was rather was stunned to discover the total waste of FAZ's elite paras, and also about the fact that Major Mahele's unit had left the critical Lualba Bridge without any protection. Sensing urgency, the French then took the decision to operate independently from the Belgians, even if in cooperation with the FAZ. Correspondingly, the responsible Belgian commander, General Claude Vanbremeersch was informed that the French intervention would commence on 20 May 1978. The French government's suggestion to postpone the operation for one day was dismissed by military commanders – at least for the moment. The only 'good news' at this point in time was the US decision to support both attempts – the French and the Belgian: obviously, somebody in Washington has decided to ignore all the differences between Paris and Brussels.

Meanwhile, the paratroopers in Calvi were ready and, indeed, eager to 'finally' go into 'real' action. Perhaps a more accurate description would be that the troops sweated with impatience: for the last few months, multiple elite units of the French military had been entrusted with external missions – like providing advisors to the Mauritanian military, or deploying support companies to Chad. The 3rd Marine Infantry Parachute Regiment (*3e Régiment de Parachutistes d'Infanterie de Marine,* 3e RPIMa) was sent almost in its full strength to Lebanon as part of a UN peace-keeping force. However, except for a few officers and NCOs, nobody from the 2e REP has seen 'action'.

The commander of the 11th Airborne Division had exploited

A rare photo of one of FAZA's C-130Hs (registration 9T-TCF) at N'Djili IAP, while being prepared to take paratroopers of the 2e REP, early on the morning of 19 May 1978. (Mark Lepko Collection)

this opportunity to gather all of his officers inside the Hall of Honour (named after the late commander of the 2nd Battalion, killed in Indochina, Commandant Barthelemy Remy Raffalli) for a 'motivational speech'. In typically French fashion, he told them that they had to be ready all the time, that the 'clouds are gathering on the political horizon, especially in Africa', and that a major crisis might erupt at any moment: 'France wants to do everything to extinguish it'. Furthermore, he informed them that the higher political and military authorities of the nation were fully aware about the sensibility of deployment of a de-facto 'mercenary' force in Africa, like the 2e REP.

Belgian Treachery?

It was at around the same time that the Belgian media revealed the completely accurate information about Brussels' intention to deploy 1,100 Belgian Para-Commandos to Zaire – including a 'spot-on' detail about the use of C-130H Hercules transports of the 15th Wing Belgian Air Force, forward deployed to Kamina AB, in southern Zaire. Knowing there were FNLC-supporters living in the Belgian capital, the French were furious: from their standpoint, this was the final straw, one that put any chance of a joint action in Kolwezi completely out of the question.

There were good reasons for the French anger. Available intelligence on the FNLC was scarce to a degree where planners of the 2e REP were forced to assume that the insurgents would be controlling all the crucial points and installations around Kolwezi – without knowing what is actually the case. In turn, later on, this led to one of the biggest controversies surrounding this entire affair: one of the never-ending arguments between French and Belgian historians writing about the Kolwezi crisis is the supposed 'disappearance' of the FNLC's regulars before the start of the French intervention. Before launching their operation, the French did not trust such rumours even if, obviously, the fact that the insurgents would be withdrawing from the town before an intervention was even launched, meant that no intervention was actually necessary – and then the Belgians were right to opt for a 'humanitarian mission'.

A detailed view of a Legionnaire in the process of filling magazines of his MAT-49 sub-machine gun. (Albert Grandolini Collection)

While true to a certain extent – then most of the FNLC subsequently encountered by the French were actually local supporters and 'irregulars', primarily from the Manika District – this is actually a legend launched by diverse Belgian sources. Although

Legionnaires sorting out their arms and other equipment on the tarmac of N'Djili IAP, in front of a DC-8 transport, on the morning of 19 May 1978. (French Ministry of Defence)

Paras lined up and ready to embark Zairian C-130Hs for their jump on Kolwezi. (French Ministry of Defence)

their bulk was withdrawn, the FNLC was still present as of 19 May, and later on, and it was quite well armed, including several AML armoured cars, heavy machine guns and plenty of assault rifles. It was rather that their commanders withdrew most of their regular units out of fear these would be destroyed by the French. Mounted on a miscellany of military and civilian vehicles captured and requisitioned, these were sent in the direction of the Angolan and Zambian borders.[61]

Enter the Leopard

From the point of view of the French, the speed of execution of the enterprise code-named Operation *Leopard* was the Priority No 1, and, indeed, they all rushed to the work with amazing determination. At 0045hrs of 18 May, the 2e REP was put on alert to be ready to move at 0300hrs. Then all the elements were moved by truck from Calvi via 175 kilometres of mountain roads to the Air Base 126, Solenzara. At 1400, the first troops boarded four DC-8s and a Boeing 707, which took off in the direction of Zaire, minutes later. With them, the paras carried only their personal armament and ammunition: their parachutes were left behind because the FAZ agreed to provide its own equipment instead. At 1800, the headquarters of the provisional transport wing responsible for Operation *Leopard* was re-deployed from Orleans to Solenzara AB, where it boarded one of COTAM's DC-8.

The first airliner carrying paratroopers of the 2e REP landed at

A nice study of one of FAZA's C-130Hs, as used to bring the 2e REP's paratroopers to Kolwezi. At least one of the Zairian Hercules' suffered a punctured tyre on first attempt to take-off from N'Djili, while another lost the way underway to Kolwezi. (Albert Grandolini Collection)

N'Djili IAP at 2315hrs local time of 18 May 1978. It was followed by the other four airliners within the following 45 minutes. By midnight, everybody was transferred to the military side of the airport. The next two hours, the paratroopers spent checking their equipment, sorting out ammunition, radios and batteries for three days of combat operations. Once everybody was kitted up, there as very little room left for bags with food rations.

At 0300hrs of 19 May 1978, a major briefing for the para-drop on Kolwezi took place in the presence of the French Ambassador Ross and Colonel Grass. The plan for the jump was quite simple – all provided everything would go smoothly. By 0400hrs, related orders were dispatched to all the involved units, FAZA's air crews and support elements. At 0600hrs, as the sun began to rise over Kinshasa, the paratroopers were provided with US made T-10 parachutes from FAZ's stocks. For nearly everybody involved, this was the first ever jump using US-made equipment. The latter had to be subjected to extensive checks, because the Zairians neglected to regularly maintain their parachutes: this resulted in the conclusion that additional improvisation was necessary in order to fit US-made parachutes to standard French harnesses. This issue was solved by using plenty of rolls of electrical tape.

Once this process was ready, the paras began embarking upon FAZA's C-130Hs – a type of aircraft from which they had never jumped before. It was at this point in time that it turned out that all the Zairian pilots went absent without a leave: the French took two hours to find them and bring them straight into the cockpits of the waiting Hercules'. The paras were then piled – somewhat haphazardly – into the aircraft. However, hardly had the first Zairian

This image, composed of multiple reconnaissance photographs, shows an aerial view of the Kolwezi 'Small' and the drop zone immediately north of the town. (Albert Grandolini Collection)

transport finally reached the runway, it burst a tyre and had to abandon the take-off. All the aircraft returned to the tarmac of the military complex on the northern side of N'Djili. Without wasting additional time, French officers then took their Legionnaires out of the aircraft and told them to push their way into the remaining five machines. Thus, the remaining four C-130Hs took off at 1100hrs for a journey to Kolwezi, each stuffed-full with 80 paratroopers carrying strange parachutes – although they were designed to take only 66 men. Slightly later, a single C.160 Transall followed them: this aircraft served as an airborne command post. Despite all the problems, the formation was thus airborne less than 12 hours after the landing of the first civilian transport that brought the Legionaries from Corsica.[62]

Jump into Kolwezi

Underway to Kolwezi, one of FAZA's C-130s lost its way: the crew spent most of the following hour to find its correct route again. The remaining three C-130Hs and the sole C.160 continued without it, nevertheless. Meanwhile, the paras – who travelled all the time sitting on their main parachute, emergency parachute, and backpacks – experienced several rapid changes of temperature inside the cargo holds of the transports. At first, the Zairian crews turned on the air conditioning, and the temperature descended nearly to the freezing point. Upon corresponding requests, the air conditioning was turned off, but this resulted in the aircraft becoming unbearably hot. With most of the troops being awake for most of the last three days, this only increased their fatigue. Finally, the aircraft reached their destination at 1430hrs, overflew the drop zone, turned around and then came back to start the drop, their crews turning on the green lights inside the cargo holds.

The first combat jump of the 2e REP since 1954 began on 19 May 1978, at 1540hrs, from an altitude of about 200 metres (650ft). The selected drop zone was some 1,000 metres (1,100 yards) from the objective. However, for unexplained reasons, the Zairian pilots dropped the French paratroops directly onto the objective. Weather conditions were anything other than ideal: strong wind from the west quickly dispersed the paras over a large area: some landed in private gardens, on the rooftops of nearby buildings, on the top of the railroad station, or somewhere in the vast fields of six-to-ten-feet-tall elephant grass and termite hills. Indeed, one of the anti-tank sections got entirely lost for the critical first 24 hours. Nevertheless, only four fractures and two sprains were reported.

First Blood

There are very different accounts of the FNLC's reaction to the appearance of hundreds of parachutists in the sky low over Kolwezi. Some of the Legionnaires reported that they had been taken under inaccurate fire while still gliding towards the ground; others landed without encountering any kind of resistance. What is certain is that, once on the ground, all three companies of the 2e REP reported being ready for action within 15 minutes. The 3rd Company was the first to open fire: upon landing, it took positions around the crossroad in the town centre where it encountered four insurgent-operated machine-guns. Having only two machine-guns on hand, the Legionnaires requested support in the form of a team equipped with LRAC F1s. As these were brought into position, three armoured cars were sighted speeding in their direction: most likely, these were all the AMLs the FNLC had managed to capture from the FAZ, and then made operational. Corporal Moran destroyed the first with a well-aimed shot from the LRAC, then quickly re-loaded and hit the second vehicle. The crew of the third AML beat a hasty retreat. This proved to be the decisive engagement: after it, the insurgents offered rather lukewarm resistance.

Meanwhile, one of the platoons of the 3rd Company entered the Hotel Impala – only to find 24 pairs of hands, tied and then cut off from white people, presumably expatriates, and then the bodies of 20 dead locals. Kolwezi was a town with a large percentage of internal immigrants from other parts of Zaire, and it seems that the FNLC's political officers not only suspected most of these, but treated them as 'collaborators of colonialists', or at least 'loyal to Mobutu'. Therefore, they were declared 'legitimate targets' of a vendetta for FAZ-instigated massacres from 1977.

Having positioned its sniper section, equipped with brand-new F1 sniper rifles, on the roof of the Saint Mary Cathedral, another platoon from the 3rd Company secured the road to the Manika District. Elite sharpshooters then methodically eliminated any FNLC unwise enough to show up, usually by hits from around 300 metres. Following a short exchange of fire with insurgents, the paras then entered the Technical College, adjacent to Manika, where they found 26 Europeans and 9 Congolese – alive. This was only the first example of the Legionnaires directly freeing hostages of the FNLC during the campaign. When questioned, the hostages quickly confirmed that the core of the FNLC's regulars has left Kolwezi ahead of the intervention, and that the majority of the armed insurgents still in the town were – increasingly panicky – 'irregulars'.

A still from a video showing one of the AMLs captured by the FNLC and then knocked out by a LRAC-team of the 3rd Company, 2e REP. (Mark Lepko Collection)

A Legionnaire sniper with one of the then brand-new F1 sniper rifles, inside Kolwezi. (Albert Grandolini Collection)

In the meantime, the 1st Company secured the John XXIII High School and the area between the two lakes south of the town centre. There the French troops discovered the scattered bodies of many of the FNLC's victims – white and black alike. Grim pictures of this scene quickly found their way to the international press. The 2nd Company encountered only isolated pockets of resistance during its landing and the following advance on the GECAMINES Hospital. Whatever was in the way was 'neutralized like on the training field', according to one of the NCOs involved. The Legionnaires were less pleased about what they found inside the GECAMINES' garage: most of the trucks and other potentially useful vehicles there were deliberately sabotaged by the FNLC – probably even before the insurgency had reached the town.

Operation *Red Bean*

Conscious that their heavy weapons and vehicles were about to arrive with the second flight, the paras spent the night rapidly digging in and resting. With there being only little resistance on the ground, when the four C-130s and a lone C.160 arrived overhead with further men from the 2e REP, Erulin decided that the situation did not warrant the risk of a night jump. Therefore, the aircraft were sent off to Lubumbashi, whence they returned at dawn to drop the men of the 4th Company in a successful second jump. Immediately after landing, the 4th Company assaulted the new town from the east: whatever insurgents were still around were taken by surprise and unable to react. The area was secured in a matter of a few hours.

With Kolwezi being completely silent, and all neuralgic spots under their firm control, the paras were able to concentrate on looking for expatriates. They first checked the White Rectangle and the GECAMINES settlement. The only clash with the FNLC took place around 0700hrs, on the fringes of the Mainka District, and involved the troops of the 3rd Company 2e REP. Shortly after, Captain Gaussers spotted several unidentified vehicles approaching the positions of his troops. Quickly recognizing who it was, he sarcastically commented in not the last diplomatic fashion, 'Merde, voila, les Belges!'

Indeed, it was at this point in time that the Belgians finally began showing up. Thus, it is also the moment to take a closer look at how they had organized their intervention. Although Brussels was receiving quite accurate intelligence about the developments inside Kolwezi – including precise information about the withdrawal of most of FNLC's regulars – there was simply no decision-making chain between their military and civilian authorities. Instead, the feeling of not precisely knowing what to do began to spread within both circles, and this was only increased when overcautious Belgian politicians began meddling – often to the level of absurdity.[63]

Despite excellent intelligence, the Belgian military vastly overestimated the strength of the FNLC in Kolwezi, and thus its Para-Commandos – commanded by Colonel Rik Deporter – were briefed to expect up to 4,000 well armed insurgents. Like their French colleagues, Deporter's staff planned to land in two separate zones: elements of the 2nd (including the 14th Company) and 3rd Battalions (including the 15th and 17th Companies), commanded by Major G Couwenberg were to seize the 'Small' airfield north of the town, and then evacuate expatriates in the quickest possible fashion.

Knowing that a 22-hour ride on C-130s would fatigue his 1,171 paras, Deporter had them being flown to Kamina AB on board two Boeing 727s and eight Boeing 707 of Sabena, the Belgian national airline. Overflight problems caused the Belgians to travel along the route from Madeira to Abijan and then to Liberville. The airliners were followed by eight C-130Hs of the Belgian Air force, which carried a cargo of 28 jeeps and 26 AS.24 tricycles (which were to prove very useful in the following action), ammunition, and a full field hospital, while one flew in a priceless tool: an Alouette helicopter, which was assembled upon landing.[64]

At Kamina, the Belgians quickly re-assembled their force and then flew to Kolwezi 'Main' on board their C-130Hs: these arrived over the town about half an hour after the landing of the second French wave – and then simply landed. Once on the ground, the Belgian para-commandos quickly secured the airport, where they found a handful of survivors from the 311th Parachute Battalion FAZ.

Legionnaire paras of the 'second wave' – the 4th Company, 2e REP – under their parachutes – outside Kolwezi, at dawn of 21 May 1978. (Albert Grandolini Collection)

Paras from a group that has already assembled amid the elephant grass, watching as the rest of the 4th Company descends. (Albert Grandolini Collection)

Legionnaires advancing through the backyards of Kolwezi. Note the prominent MAT-49 submachine gun in the hands of the Legionnaire nearest to the camera (Albert Grandolini Collection)

One of the Boeing 707s of the Belgian national airline Sabena, used to transport Belgian para-commandos to Kamina AB, in western Zaire. (Belgian Ministry of Defence)

Peculiarities of Franco-Belgian Cooperation

The landing of Belgian C-130Hs at Kolwezi 'Main' was monitored by an increasingly concerned Colonel Grass, underway on board the C.160 that acted as his airborne command post: clearly, due to the lack of coordination there was a latent danger of a 'friendly fire' incident between the two nominally friendly forces.[65]

However, on the ground, the cooperation functioned nearly flawlessly, and that right from the start. Once he recognized the identity of the troops approaching his position, Captain Gaussers came forward – to meet his Belgian counterpart, Captain De Wulf, from the 17th Company, 3rd Battalion of the Para-Commando Regiment. The two knew each other from earlier joint operations in Africa and thus quickly started a chat – during which they found out that their objectives were entirely different. Agreeing to disagree, each wished other the best of luck, and then they parted.

Elsewhere, first encounters between the Belgians and the French were less friendly: indeed, some of these resulted in brief skirmishes. By sheer luck, nobody was injured – despite the presence of plenty of 'trigger happy' troops on both sides. The principal reason was that almost everybody involved expected to encounter Angolan or Cuban troops on the FNLC's side. Indeed, diverse of local sources even reported the presence of at least one 'white' officer or NCO within the insurgent ranks. Such claims were subsequently all dismissed: the person in question simply turned out to be an indigenous albino – an anomaly not at all uncommon in the Congo or, indeed, in all of Sub-Saharan Africa.

On the contrary, subsequent Franco-Belgian cooperation in Kolwezi actually proceeded smoothly and was characterised by the quick completion of the tactical aims of both parties. The reason for this was a meeting between Grass and Deporter in the course of which the Belgian told his French colleague that the Belgians couldn't care less about what exactly was going on in Kolwezi, as long as they could complete the evacuation of the expatriates. The two thus agreed a set of measures aimed at avoidance of a direct contact and thus any kind of undesirable confrontations. Immediately afterwards, Grass ordered the 2e REP to withdraw from nearly all the points around the town, except for Manika and the railway crossing: in this fashion, they were to enable the Para-Commandos to quickly find and assemble all the expatriates and move them to the 'Main' airfield – and straight to awaiting aircraft that flew them out to Kigali, in Rwanda. Indeed, the French then went as far as to do favours for Deporter, in that they provided the same FAZA transports to the Belgians as flew the 2e REP into Kolwezi, in order to speed up the rescue operation. In turn, the Belgians permitted the French to make use of their field hospital on board one of 15th Wing's Hercules.

Metal Shaba

Good cooperation between the Belgian para-commandos and the French Legionnaires was necessary also because, starting around the noon of 20 May 1978, the FAZA's Mirages re-appeared in the sky over Kolwezi. According to recollections of the French personnel involved, these flew no air strikes on the day of the jump, 'only reconnaissance and a token show of force'. However, for 20 May, Bour recalled:

> Operational intelligence from Legionnaire paratroopers and other forces in Kolwezi enabled them to start providing air support. Indeed, during the day the Mirages attacked several truck

Suspected FNLC loyalist in Kolwezi caught by the paras of the 2e REP: his hideout was revealed by the locals. (via Daniel Kowalczuk)

A Legionnaire from the 4th Company (the only ones to wear camouflage uniforms during the Shaba II) 'entering' a suspect home inside Kolwezi. (Albert Grandolini Collection)

Mortar team of the 2e REP with their weapon in position within the Camp Forrest, north-east of Kolwezi. (Albert Grandolini Collection)

Legionnaires aboard a requisitioned civilian truck underway outside the town of Kolwezi. Vehicles like this one were found within the GECAMINES compound, repaired and then quickly put into action. (Albert Grandolini Collection)

columns carrying withdrawing insurgents. One of the involved pilots attacked three vehicles spotted south of the metallurgical plant owned by the Société Metallurgique du Katanga (formerly METALKAT, then Metal-Shaba). The vehicles were then subjected to heavy mortar fire from the French paratroopers, which all but destroyed the small convoy, leaving few survivors to flee north. Guided by an Alouette III helicopter, a Mirage 5M made a firing pass on the insurgents on the road to Kazenze, too.

The action in the area of the Metal Shaba mine was initiated by the 4th Company 2e REP on the morning of 20 May, when its scouts identified a significant presence of about 300 uniformed FNLC troops. As the Legionnaires bumped into insurgents, the latter counter-attacked, using lorry-borne infantry supported by two APCs generally described as 'Soviet-built light tanks'. While one French soldier was killed and another gravely wounded, the Legionnaires hit back with all of their fire arms, machine guns and mortars. Reinforcements in the form of the 2nd Company commanded by Captain Dubos – and brought in with help of vehicles requisitioned from the GECAMINES' garage – enabled them to outflank their opponent. The Mirages then attacked from the opposite direction, using their DEFA 30mm cannons with great effect: subjected to intensive crossfire, the FNLC unit fell apart and rapidly withdrew, leaving more than 80 dead behind.

Although this clash marked the end of any kind of organized resistance of the Katangese insurgency during the Kolwezi campaign, it was an indication of the possible threat for the small French force – provided the insurgents decided to fight instead of fleeing. After it, only minor incidents involving either individuals or small groups of

FNLC loyalists and foreign troops were registered.

Mopping Up

Early on 21 May, the majority of the 2e REP arrived from Lubumbashi, with the remainder following during the course of the day. With the situation firmly under control, and the entire Beligan Para-Commando Regiment on the ground in Kolwezi, Deporter ordered his force to intensify the search for expatriates: too many Belgian families were still unaccounted for, and scattered all over the place. The Belgians thus spent the entire day concentrated on getting the expatriates out, while the French busied themselves with the darker side of the story: for the next five days the Legionnaires combed surroundings of Kolwezi for insurgents and their hostages – and the body count. Larger groups of Europeans were found rather quickly, many half-crazed with fear as a result of their harrowing experiences with the 'Tigers' and their local supporters. Others were less lucky: eventually, the bodies of over 160 murdered expatriates and 'several hundred' of the Congolese were found.

A column of jeep-mounted Belgian para-commandos waiting for the order to move out from Kolwezi 'Main'. (Albert Grandolini Collection)

Belgian para-commandos at one of GECAMINES' facilities. (Albert Grandolini Collection)

The evacuation of expatriates began during the evening of 21 May. Two Boeing 727-100s of the 15th Wing of the Belgian Air Force led the procession, and were soon reinforced by the British and Italians: three Hercules C.Mk 1 and a VC-10 configured as a flying hospital of the Royal Air Force flew in a medical team and supplies from Lusaka in Zambia, while an Italian Air Force C-130H brought in food. Eventually, the transports of the Belgian Air Force flew 32 roundtrip sorties between Brussels and Kamina, and 426 'local' sorties by C-130, logging a staggering 1,726 hours of flying time in just four days. Some of their pilots logged 30 hours of flying time during this period. The AdA flew at least 2,300 hours in seven days, many of which included hauling ammunition from depots in Chad and other French garrisons in Africa. Overall, their and US transports helped deliver 4,000 infantry troops to Zaire, and fly out 2,300 hostages.

Meanwhile, the USAF began supporting this operation too. The start was made by four Lockheed C-141A Star Lifters that brought in 352 tonnes of fuel, because the fuel farm at Kamina AB was non-operational, on 21 May. Eventually, a total of 18 such aircraft and Lockheed C-5As became involved in bringing in additional French and Belgian equipment, and shifting fuel and supplies from Kinshasa to Kolwezi. The fuel and parking ramp space-related problems forced the USAF to move its forward operational base from Monrovia in Liberia to Dakar in Senegal. Eventually, US transports brought in 100 tonnes of cargo from Brussels to Kamina AB, while the 2e REP was supported through delivery of 437 tonnes of cargo and 120 personnel to Lubumbashi.[66]

The 2e REP continued mopping up in and around Kolwezi for a few days longer, before leaving the town to Belgian control. The few FNLC still inside the town were either killed or captured, and only a very few managed to follow the regulars that retreated into Angola. Behind them, the town was in a shambles: there was no electricity, most of the infrastructure was destroyed and following the evacuation of the Belgian cadre of the GECAMINES, the entire mining industry of Zaire was about to collapse. Hungry for media

One of the giant Lockheed C-5A Galaxy transports of the US Air Force about to unload heavy equipment for the French and Belgian contingents at N'Djili IAP. (US DoD)

USAF C-141s loading trucks with spare tyres and other supplies for French and Belgian troops involved in Operations *Leopard* and *Red Bean*. (US DoD)

Flight personnel and staff of the 15th Wing of the Belgian Air Force in front of the C-130H 'CH-01', after successful conclusion of the Operation *Red Bean*. Some of pilots in question have clocked up to 30 hours of flight time within only four days. (US DoD)

attention, and willing to milk somebody else's effort, Mobutu arrived to visit the place: he was visibly shaken by the sight of the many corpses presented to him. Otherwise, the Zairian strongman and his military proved of little value. Therefore, Grass visited Erulin to let him know that the Legionnaires were to stay in Kolwezi for a while longer, and help re-establish the rule of law – not only in the town, but in all of the Shaba, too. Correspondingly, using trucks flown in by US transport aircraft, different elements of the 2e REP moved ever further away from the town: one company made for Kapata, in the south-west, and another for Luilu to the north, where some of scattered insurgents were rounded up. During one of these operations, three parachutists were ambushed and killed by insurgents. In return, between 23 and 26 May, the French troops claimed to have killed several dozens of insurgents in

Late into action, FAZA's MB.326s did attempt to 'punish' the withdrawing insurgents. This still from a video shows one of them in the process of being re-armed with 68mm unguided rockets for Matra F2 pods. (Albert Grandolini Collection)

A still from the same video, showing the fully loaded Matra F2 pod. (Albert Grandolini Collection)

places as far as 100 kilometres away from Kolwezi. The insurgents suffered additional casualties to air strikes of FAZA's MB.326s: after being forward-deployed to Kolwezi 'Main' under the command of Colonel Ikuku Luiza they quickly flew up to 50 combat sorties: it is unknown if any of the pilots involved complained this time. The FAZ suffered losses to their air strikes too: in one of the final combat operations, flown on 1 June 1978, a lonesome MB.326GB hit a column of troops advancing along the railway line near Dilolo. A few other air strikes hit diverse objects inside Angola, too.

First In, First Out

The last laugh in the Franco-Belgian banter – of which there was quite a lot in those days – was to be one of the Foreign Legion. Although the Operation *Red Bean* was officially completed on the evening of 21 May, the Para-Commando Regiment then received the order to leave one of its battalions in Kolwezi – with the purpose of completing the evacuation of remaining expatriates, serving as a police, and helping in the work of restoring and maintaining local installations. The Belgian Para-Commandos, who were supposed to go in, evacuate the expatriates and then go out, thus had to watch in the murky mood as their French 'comrades' embarked USAF transports that flew them back to their base on Corsica. Namely,

Armament specialists pushing a cart with additional unguided rockets and 50kg bombs. (Albert Grandolini Collection)

after eight days of continuous action, the 2e REP was ordered to return to Kolwezi 'Main', on 6 June, and disengage. By the time, it lost five troops killed and 25 wounded, while eliminating about 250 insurgents and wounding 170.

Eventually, the 1st Para Commando Battalion remained in Zaire for more than a month: on 25 June 1978 it was relieved by the 3rd Battalion, which continued carrying out pretty much the same responsibilities.

Furthermore, the Belgians took over the responsibility for reorganizing and re-training the FAZ – especially its shaken paratroopers. After all, not only II Shaba War has clearly exposed inherent weaknesses of the Zairian military: except for paratroopers, most of the FAZ units tended to flee whenever coming under fire. Similarly, while crews of transport- and helicopter-units did their utmost to provide support – for their won ground forces, but also those of foreign armies – the Mirage-squadron managed only a handful of sorties, and most of these were either ineffective, or entirely missed their targets.

Certainly enough, the Belgians were not left alone in their efforts to rebuild the FAZ. Communist China provided advisors required to train a new, brigade-sized 'crack' commando unit, while the MMF was contracted to create a 'Rapid Reaction Brigade' of the FAZ.

African Peace-Keeping Force

Despite all the aid he has received from France, Belgium and the USA, Mobutu became increasingly nervous over the extended presence of 'colonial' military forces in his country. Therefore, Paris, Brussels and Washington began to search for a way out. The Moroccans reacted as first, and promised to deploy 1,500 of their troops. Over the following days, these were complemented by approximately a battalion of troops from Senegal, one company from Gabon and Togo each, and a medical unit from Ivory Coast: while Moroccans were deployed to Kolwezi on board US transports, others travelled on board of US C-141s and Belgian C-130s: US transports alone are known to have flown in 1,214 tonnes of related cargo and 416 personnel. Thus came into being the Inter-African Force, totalling about 2,500 officers and other ranks.

Burned out wreck of a FAZA Alouette III helicopter as found at Kolwezi 'Main'. (French Ministry of Defence)

Wreckage of the MB.326GB serial FG-468 and two light aircraft at Kolwezi 'Main'. (French Ministry of Defence)

The boom and the fin of the sole FAZA SA.330 Puma found by the FNLC and then destroyed at Kolwezi. Visible in the rear is one of the Transalls of the French Air Force. (Albert Grandolini Collection)

The Inter-African Force was withdrawn only in mid-1979, when the threat of a possible III Shaba War vanished in the thin and hot savannah air. It passed the control over Kolwezi and the region to the retrained FAZ units.

By then the official count of casualties was complete. According to the Zairian Red Cross and the International Committee of the Red Cross, 855 people were killed during the II Shaba War. Between them were 136 expatriates: most were Europeans, but also a few Libyans and Pakistanis that worked in Kolwezi and were executed because the insurgents mistook them for Moroccans. At least 300 Zairian civilians were massacred as well, including 85 women. About 419 fatalities included either FAZ officers and other ranks, or about 250 insurgents, who also lost 1,000 diverse assault rifles, 48 heavy- and light machine guns, four recoilless guns, and 15 mortars, 21 rocket launchers. That said, even official Kinshasa subsequently confirmed that the actual number of deaths is likely to be higher, because many of casualties have been buried privately.[67]

The material and financial damage for Zaire was far more massive. The government not only spent colossal amounts of money for its two intervention, but after the II Shaba War found the economy at a standstill and unlike to get moving again for quite a while: it took at least three months to replace the majority of the European technicians that used to work in the Shaba mines. Other sectors were heavily hit too: almost all the cotton, peanut and corn fields in the Shaba have been burned by the insurgents in 1977, and produced next to nothing. The insurgents also looted all agricultural material of the Commission Agricole du Shaba, took away nearly all of the livestock in Lualba district, destroyed seven bridges and one ferry boat during Shaba II. All the hospitals and schools in south-western Shaba were looted,

Zairian troops inspecting abandoned civilian cars around Kolwezi. (Albert Grandolini Collection)

Mounted on a requisitioned civilian truck, this group of FAZ troops was photographed while arriving in Kolwezi – as they passed by a shot-up VW Beetle. (Albert Grandolini Collection)

French paras waiting for their embarkation on USAF transports that returned them home. (Albert Grandolini Collection)

Legionnaires hauling away a recoilless gun left behind by the FNLC. (Albert Grandolini Collection)

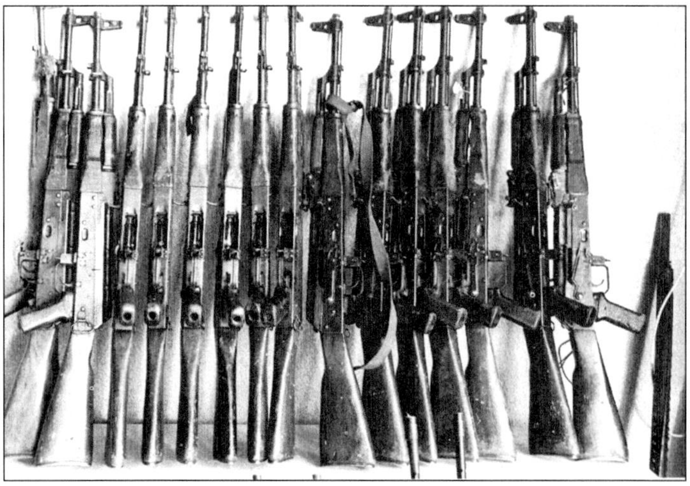

A line of AK-47 and AKM assault rifles captured by the 2e REP during Shaba II. (Albert Grandolini Collection)

Two para-commandos inspecting an abandoned civilian vehicle outside Kolwezi. (Albert Grandolini Collection)

A C-130H of the FAZA unloading vehicles of the African peace-keeping force. (Albert Grandolini Collection)

ruined or destroyed, and the railroad between Dilolo and Lobito (in Angola) was damaged in several places in 1977 and 1978. Overall, the complete material damage was estimated at US$3.035 million.[68]

With hindsight it can be concluded that Zaire never recovered from the crippling blow delivered by the FNLC during Shaba II. Unsurprisingly, Mobutu subsequently took good care to re-negotiate the deals with Angolans, and make sure that a status quo would be maintained. With hindsight, it can be said that the related talks resulted in a peace that was to last until his downfall, in 1997: not only that Zaire ceased supporting the FNLA and the FLEC, but also Angola never left the FNLC launch another attack into Shaba.

CHAPTER 7
CONCLUSIONS

A complete summary of the Operations *Leopard* and *Red Bean* ought to start with pointing out the amazing speed with which the 2e REP was prepared for action, deployed to Zaire, and then executed its combat jump. Despite their rather sluggish approach early on, the Belgians proved well-prepared, too. Both forces were supported by an adequate logistic tail. If at all, one could criticise the Belgians for rescuing hostages in a 'little bit too perfect fashion', and thus in only a slightly slower way than the French could do.

What had been most definitely proven during the Kolwezi Crisis was the total incompetence and inability of the FAZ (and Mobutu) to mount a rapid reaction in the case of a major crisis. The Zairian military, which earned itself an 'above the African average' reputation was rather quickly blown away – and then not only in May 1978: actually, this had happened already a year before, when the FAZ could not operate without Moroccan and Egyptian help. What is ironic about this is that the FNLC actually never had a chance of separating Shaba from Zaire – at least not for any protracted period of time: there is little doubt that even if one of its two attempts to do so would have been successful, European powers, and probably the USA too, would have launched a military intervention in favour of Mobutu, simply because of their economic interests. Unsurprisingly, while Shaba I failed to do so, Shaba II did the trick: it forced the Zairian strongman to significantly downsize his support for the FNLA and the FLEC. In the case of the former, this proved to be the killing blow: already split into several factions, subsequently this group played no role in the Angolan War.

As time was to show, although 'reformed' time and again, and despite having its military 're-trained' by the Belgians, French, the Chinese, and even the Israelis during the 1980s, Mobutu's Zaire was to survive for about 20 years longer. During the I Congo War of 1996-1997, the FAZ quickly succumbed to a Rwandan-led invasion. Following Mobutu's downfall, the country came under the rule of Laurent Kabila – once a small-time leftist revolutionary, cum wealthy businessman, who established himself in power as a leader of a Rwandan-supported alliance of several minor insurgent groups. However, by 1998, Kabila split with the Rwandans and began leaning upon an alliance between members of his ethnic groups and the Katangese, in turn prompting Kigali to launch a new invasion and thus spark the II Congo War, which was to last until at least 2001. Combined, the I and the II Congo War – the latter is often cited as the 'I African War', too, because it involved militaries from about a dozen different countries from that continent – were by far the bloodiest conflicts ever fought in Africa. Although its troops and diverse proxies established themselves in control of more than half of the Congo, Rwanda and Uganda were defeated by an Angolan-Zimbabwean-led alliance towards the end of that conflict. Nevertheless, ever since the various Rwandan proxies continue to destabilise the huge country by continuous mutinies and uprisings.

Mobutu's legacy is thus one of a never-ending war in a country that has known little other than war ever since its independence. Nevertheless, historians have never sorted him into the same category as Ugandan strongman Idi Amin or mad and cannibalistic 'Emperor' of Central Africa, Jean-Bédel Bokassa. Rather than this, Mobutu is usually cited as an example of a 'friendly dictator' and 'lesser evil' from the times of the Cold War. Similarly, only a few want to recall that his long reign over Congo/Zaire only became possible precisely because foreign powers were insistent on looking away while he and his clique were mismanaging the country and massacring thousands of oppositionals for reasons officially related to 'higher national interests' of the West – effectively the commercial interests of diverse privately owned Western corporations. It is almost tragic that such aspects are entirely ignored in nearly every study of the Operations *Leopard* and *Red Bean* too: instead, the Franco-Belgian intervention remains memorised for its achievement in regards of white expatriates first and foremost – as the 'Rescue at Kolwezi' – until this very day.

APPENDIX I
Killed and wounded Soldiers of the 2e REP in Kolwezi

Dead:
Sergent-chef Daniel KIA
Caporal Arnold KIA
Legionnaire Clement KIA
Caporal Harte KIA
Caporal-chef Allioui KIA

Wounded:
1st Company 2e REP: Legionnaire Marco; Caporal Pain; Legionnaire Soral
2nd Company 2e REP: Sergent Cabrol; Caporal Ovacick; Caporal Dallet; Lieutenant Raymond; Caporal Bareda; Caporal-chef Senekovic; Legionnaire Seeger
3rd Company 2e REP: Legionnaire Forestier; Legionnaire Rodriguez; Legionnaire Svoboda; Caporal Courson
4th Company 2e REP: Legionnaire Jakovic; Caporal Prudence
Reconnaissance Company (CAE) 2e REP: Corporal Munoz; Legionnaire Becker; Legionnaire Gilbert
Mortars and Anti-Tank Company (CCS) 2e REP: Legionnaire Gilbert

(Note: the names given are probably not the genuine names of the soldiers, but '*nom de guerres*'; the true nationality of the troops in question was never made public, because the Legion is their 'home' and serves France)

APPENDIX II
Members of the French military assistance group in Zaire murdered on 13 May 1978 (ranks in French)

Lieutenant Jaques Laissac (born 17 June 1942): anti-tank weaponry specialist; in Zaire since 01 April 1978 on a two-year contract.
Adjudant-Chef Pierre Van Neuvel (born 11 May 1934): Armoured car maintenance specialist; in Zaire since 18 July 1976 on a two-year contract.
Adjutant Jacques Bireau (born 02 November 1942): Armoured car weapons maintenance specialist; in Zaire since 07 January 1977.
Adjutant Jaques Gomilla (born 28 January 1947): Spanish origin, armoured car maintenance specialist; in Zaire since 25 June 1976 on a two-year contract.
Adjutant Bernard Laurent (born 25 January 1942): Armoured car maintenance specialist; in Zaire since 08 January 1977.
Christian Cesario (born 01 July 1950 in French Tunisia): Helicopter electrical systems specialist; in Zaire 25 June 1977 on a two-year contract.

APPENDIX III
Weapons of the Kolwezi Crisis

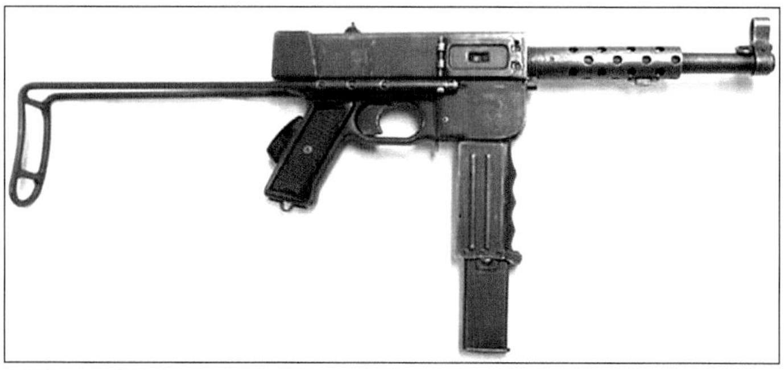

MAT-49 SMG
A nearly thirty-year-old design that had seen extensive use in Indochina and Algeria, the MAT-49 was still the weapon of choice of many veteran Foreign Legion Paras. One unusual feature of the weapon was the ability to fold the magazine forwards, underneath and parallel to the barrel. Kolwezi was the last large-scale operation where the MAT-49 was used in combat. (via Daniel Kolwaczuk)

Whilst taken in Chad during one of the Legion's many exercises there, this scene is reminiscent of the Shaba countryside in May 1978 – and shows a Legionnaire with a MAT-49. (via Daniel Kowalczuk)

FR F1 Sniper Rifle
A sniper from the 2e REP in position in Kolwezi. FR F1 sniper rifles, like the one in the photo, were responsible for most of the FNLC casualties during Operation *Leopard*. The design was based upon that of the MAS M-1936 bolt-action rifle, although only a few parts of the original rifle were interchangeable with those of the FR F1. Wooden spacers were provided for the length of the stock to be increased to suit the specific individual shooter. (Courtesy forgottenweapons.com)

Franchi LF.57 Submachine Gun
Although confirmed as being in the FNLC's arsenal, the LF.57 submachinegun saw very little combat service during the Shaba I and Shaba II. Exported to numerous African countries, such as Nigeria (during Civil War with Biafra 1967-1970), Congo-Brazzaville (ex-French Congo) and Congo/Zaire, there is a strong possibility that the actual batch in Kolwezi was the remains of the *Armee Katangaise* weapons, captured by the ANC in 1963 and kept at the FAZ's Kolwezi HQ. (via Daniel Kowalczuk)

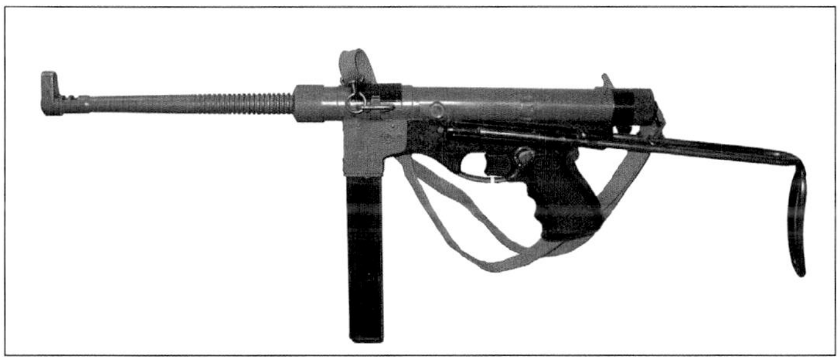

Vigneron SMG
The relatively small, simple and light weight Vigneron SMG was a highly popular weapon. The Vigneron was designed by retired colonel of the Belgian military police – turned politician Georges Vigneron, and was based essentially upon the American M3 "Grease Gun". The Vigneron SMG was particularly popular with the paras because of its folding stock, which shortened the weapon's overall length to a very convenient 24 inches (approx. 60cm). One unusual feature, albeit one also shared by the MAT-49, was that the weapon could only be discharged if the rear of the pistol grip was firmly depressed. (via Daniel Kowalczuk)

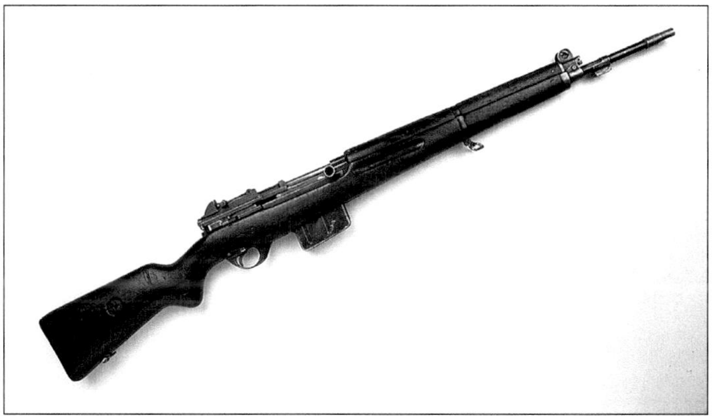

SAFN Model 49 rifle
The SAFN Model 49, inherited from the *Force Publique*, was still available to the FAZ in large numbers, but had largely been replaced by more advanced assault rifles as of 1978. More and more units were using FN-FAL automatic rifles, but the average Zairean soldier still relied on SAFN rifles, some models of which featured a bayonet lug. (via Daniel Kowalczuk)

APPENDIX IV
Flying Units involved in Shaba Wars, 1977-1978

AA (French Air Force)	Aircraft Type	Base	Role	Duration of Deployment
61 Transport Wing	Transall C.160	Orleans, Kinshasa	Transport – active participation in Operation *Leopard*	For the duration of Operation *Leopard*
UTA (Union de Transport Aeriens)				
UTA Airlines	DC-8	Deployed to Calvi and Kinshasa	Transport – active participation in Operation *Leopard*	19.05.1978 – 18.06.1978 (chartered by French Air Force for the duration of operations in Zaire during and after Operation *Leopard*
FAB (Belgian Air Force)				
20 Squadron	C-130H Hercules	Melsbroek, Kinshasa	Transport, Active participation in Operation *Red Bean*	18.05.1978 – 18.06.1978
RAF (Royal Air Force)				
Logistic Transport Wing	Hercules C.1	Lyneham, Lusaka (Zambia)	Medical supply, evacuation of British citizens	18.05.1978 – 30.05.1978
10 Squadron	VC-10 C.1	Brize Norton, Lusaka	Medical team and supply	18.05.1978 – 30.05.1978
AMI (Italian Air Force)				
50 Gruppo	C-130 Hercules	Pisa, Lusaka	Medical and food supply, evacuation of Italian citizens	18.05.1978 – 30.05.1978
USAF (United States Air Force)				
437 Military Airlift Wing	C-141A	Charleston AFB	Transport	18.05.1978 – 30.06.1978
438 Military Airlift Wing	C-141A	McGuire AFB	Transport	18.05.1978 – 30.06.1978
436 Military Airlift Wing	C-5A Galaxy	Dover AFB (United Kingdom)	Transport	18.05.1978 – 30.06.1978

BIBLIOGRAPHY

Apostolo, G., *Aermacchi MB 326* (Torino: La Bancarella Aeronautica, 1999).

Beaumont, H., *Mirage III, Mirage 5, Mirage 50: Toutes les versions en France et dans le Monde* (Clichy Cedex: Éditions Larivière 2005, ISBN 2-84890-979-2).

Bevillard, A., *La Saga du Transport Aerien Militaire Francais* (L'espirit du livre editions: 2007, ISBN 978-2-915960).

Bonnet, R-P., *Colonel Erulin – Zaire – Sauver Kolwezi* (ECPA – Erich Baschet Editions: 1980, ISBN 2-86-309-007-0).

Brackx, D., *Luchtstrijdskrachten Belgie* (Flash Aviation/ Flash Luchtvaart Winkel: 2006, ISBN 90-71553-17-5).

Braeckman, Colette, *Le Dinosaure, le Zaïre de Mobutu* (Fayard: 1992; ISBN 978-2213028637).

Brent, W., *African Air Forces* (Freeworld Publications: 1999).

Byangoy, D. M., *Dieu Merci, Le role de l'Armée dans la pacification des nations, Cas de la RDC et du Rwanda* (Université de Lubumbashi, 2011).

Chauvel, J-F., *Kolwezi – Les Secrets du Raid* (Oliver Orban: 1978, ISBN 2-85565-079-8).

Cochrane, J. & Elliott, S., *Military Aircraft Insignia of the World* (Shrewsbury: Airlife Publishing, 1998, ISBN 1-85310-873-1).

Cooper, T., *Africa@War Volume 13: Great Lakes Holocaust: The First Congo War, 1996-1997* (Solihull: Helion & Co., 2013, ISBN 978-1-909384-65-1).

Cooper, T., *Africa@War Volume 14: Great Lakes Conflagration: The Second Congo War, 1998-2003*, (Solihull: Helion & Co., 2013, ISBN 978-1-909384-66-8).

Cooper, T., Nicolle, D., with Nordeen, L., Salti, P., and Smisek, M., *Arab MiGs, Volume 4, Attrition War, 1967-1973* (Houston: Harpia Publishing, 2013, ISBN 978-09854554-1-5)

Cooper, T., Nicolle, D., with Grandolini A, Nordeen, L., and Smisek, M., *Arab MiGs, Volume 6: October 1973 War, Part 2* (Houston: Harpia Publishing, 2015, ISBN 978-0-9854554-6-0)

Delalande, A., 'Mirage Au Congo: The Dassault Mirage 5M/DM in Zaire, 1975-88', *The Aviation Historian*, Volume 18 (01-2017).

Dupuy, T. N. (Col, US Army, ret.), and Blanchard W. (Col, US Army, ret.) *The Almanac of World Military Power* (Dunn Loring/London, T. N. Dupuy Associates/Arthur Barker Ltd., 1972, ISBN 0-213-16418-3).

Flintham, V., *Air Wars and Aircraft: a Detailed Record of Air Combat 1945 to the Present* (London, Arms and Armour Press, 1989, ISBN 0-85368-779-X).

FNLC, *The Question of "Zaire"/Congo: The History of the 1977-78 Uprising in the Congo* (New York, John Brown Book Club, 1979).

Fontanellaz, A. & Cooper, T., *Africa@War Volume 31: War of Intervention in Angola: Angolan and Cuban Military, 1975-1976*, (Solihull, Helion & Co., 2018, ISBN 978-1-911628-19-4).

George, E., *The Cuban Intervention in Angola, 1965-1991, From Che Guevara to Cuito Cuanavale* (Oxon: Frank Cass, 2005; ISBN 0-415-35015-8).

Gleijeses, P., 'Truth or Credibility: Castro, Carter, and the Invasions of Shaba', *The International History Review*, Vol 18/1 (2010).

Gleijeses, P., *Conflicting Missions: Havana, Washington, and Africa, 1959-1976* (Chapel Hill: The University of North Carolina Press, 2002, ISBN 0-8078-2647-2).

Green, W. & Fricker, j., *The Air Forces of the World: Their History, Development and Present Strength* (London, MacDonald & CO, 1958).

Hudson, A., *Africa@War Volume 6: Congo Unravelled: Military Operations from Independence to the Mercenary Revolt*, 1960-68, (Solihull, Helion & Co., 2012, ISBN 978-1-907677-63-2).

Huertas, S. M., *Dassault-Breguet Mirage III/5*, (London: Osprey Publishing, 1990, ISBN 0-85045-933-8).

Jackson, P. A., *Belgian Military Aviation 1945-1977* (Midland Counties Publications, 1977, ISBN 0-904597-06-7).

Kennes, E. & Larmer M., *The Katangese Gendarmes and War in Central Africa* (Bloomington: Indiana University Press, 2016; ISBN 9780253021304).

Kennes, E., *The Democratic Republic of the Congo: Strucures of Greed, Networks of Need, Rethinking the Economics of War* (Washington: Woodrow Wilson Center, 2005).

Malu, Major M. Di, *The Shaba Invasions* (Fort Leavenworth: Master of Military Art and Science thesis, US Army Command & General Staff College, 2001).

Mamdani, M., *Good Muslim, Bad Muslim: America, the Cold War, and the Roots of Terrorism* (New York: Pantheon, 2004, ISBN 0-375-42285-4).

Morgan, *DR Congo's $24 trillion fortune*, African Business, February 2009.

Nzongola-Ntalaja, Georges, *Congo: From Leopold to Kabila: A People's History* (London: Zed Books Ltd, 2002, ISBN 978-1-84277-062-8).

Odom, Lieutenant-Colonel Thomas P., *Shaba II: the French and Belgian Intervention in Zaire in 1978* (Fort Leaenworth: US Army Command and General Staff College, 1993).

Ogunbadejo, O., 'Conflict in Africa: A Case Study of the Shaba Crisis, 1977', *World Affairs* Vol. 144/3 (Winter 1979).

Owen, J. I. H., *Infantry Weapons of the Armies of Africa, the Orient and Latin America* (Brassey's Publishers Limited, 1980, ISBN 0-8277-7388-9).

Pasierbinski, T., *Operation Leopard* (in Polish), (Polish Ministry of Defence Publishing House, 1980, ISBN 83-11-06543-8).

Sergent, P., *La Legion Saute sur Kolwezi* (France Loisirs, 1978, ISBN 2-7242-0398-4).

Sonck, J. P & Despas, D., 'L'Aviation Katangaise', *Avions* magazine, volumes 34, 35 and 36 (1996).

Sonck, J. P., 'Echec aux Simba', *Avions* magazine, volumes 97 (2001), 131 and 138 (2004).

Sonck, J. P., 'La Force Aérienne Congolaise', *Contact* magazine, volumes 39 and 40 (2005).

Sonck, J. P., 'La Force Aérienne Congolaise', *Jets* magazine, volumes 32, 33 and 34 (1998).

Sonck, J. P., 'MB 326 Sous Le Ciel Zairois', *Jets* magazine, volume 10 (1996).

Storaro, F., *1964-1984, Vent' Anni di Aeronautica Militare: Missione Africa* (Istituto Bibliografico Napoleone, Roma, 2010).

Tanks of the World: Taschenbuch der Panzer (Koblenz, Bernard & Graefe Verlag, 1990, ISBN 3-7637-5871-2).

Thompson, Sir R. (editor), *War in Peace: An Analysis of Warfare since 1945* (London: Orbis Publishing, 1981, ISBN 0-85613-341-8).

Turner, J. W., *Continent Ablaze: The Insurgency Wars in Africa 1960 to the Present* (London: Arms & Armour Press, 1998, ISBN 1-85409-128-X)

Van Nederveen, Captain Gilles K., *USAF Airlift into the Heart of Darkness, the Congo 1960-1978: Implications for Modern Air Mobility Planners* (Air University, September 2001).

Weigert, S. L., *Angola: A Modern Military History, 1961-2002* (Basingstoke: 2011).

Windrow, M & Braby, W., *French Foreign Legion Paratroopers* (London: Osprey Publishing, 1985, ISBN 0-85045-629-0).

World Defence Almanac, *Military Technology* magazine volumes 1/91, 1/93, 1/95, 1/97, 1/98 & 1/03

NOTES

1 Di Malu, p.19.
2 Ibid, p.20.
3 Ibid, p.2.
4 Ibid, p.4.
5 Thompson et all, p.144. Basic pay of every mercenary was up to GBP 180 a month, plus allowances and other inducements. In comparison, Malu cites the recruitment of up to 15,000 of 'Gendarmes'.
6 For fuller details of the mercenary operations in the Congo of the 1960s, see Hudson, *Congo Unravelled* (Africa@War Volume 6); a more detailed coverage of the Katangan military established in the 1960s is to follow in a future volume in this series.
7 Pasierbinski, p.33.
8 Unless stated otherwise, the content of this chapter is largely based on Cooper, *Great Lakes Holocaust* & Fontanellaz et al, *War of Intervention in Angola* (see Bibliography for details).
9 Interestingly, British intelligence reports had indicated that the latter groups were all not only armed, but still uniformed and operated in the form of a 'regular army', see Pasierbinski, p.144.
10 Braeckmann, pp.61, 170, 229 & Byangoy, *Le role de l'Armée dans la pacification des nations* (see Bibliography for details).
11 Braeckmann, p.61; DIA, 'Zaire, Mobutu and the Military, An intelligence Assessment', August 1982, CIA FOIA Electronic Reading Room (henceforth CIA/FOIA/ERR); Byangoy, *Le role de l'Armée dans la pacification des nations* & Desc-wondo.org, 24 September 2013.
12 CIA, 'Zaire, National Intelligence Survey, 1973', CIA/FOIA/ERR.
13 Di Malu, p.23.
14 Generally, the number of SAFN Model 49 rifles in the FAZ always remained low: the force acquired large numbers of FN-FALs, Chinese Type 56 and US-made M16s during the 1970s, and thus required no fourth type of assault rifle. Indeed, it seems that most of SAFN Model 49s ended in service with the Gendarmerie and the Civil Guard.
15 Storaro, *1964-1984*, pp.14-89; Hagedorn et all, *Foreign Invaders*, pp.148-155.
16 Storaro, *1964-1984*, p.27.
17 Ibid, p.27 & Aposotolo, pp.31-33 & Sonck, 'L'Aermacchi MB 326 Sous le ciel Zairois'.
18 Brent, pp.49-50.
19 Sonck, 'L'Aermacchi MB 326 Sous le ciel Zairois'.
20 Ibid.
21 CIA, 'Zaire, National Intelligence Survey, 1973', CIA/FOIA/ERR.
22 Sonck, 'L'Aermacchi MB 326 Sous le ciel Zairois'.
23 Ibid; Storaro, *1964-1984*, pp.51-59; *Congolese Air Force Operating MB.326GBs*, Aviation Week & Space Technology, 1971.
24 Delallande, 'Mirage au Congo'.
25 Delalande, 'Mirage au Congo'.
26 Beaumont, *Mirage III/5/50*, pp.46 & 66; Cooper et all, *Arab MiGs Volume 4*, pp.218-220; Cooper et all, *Arab MiGs Volume 6*, pp.23-24. The second 'M' in the designation of Mirage 5s manufactured for Zaire stood for 'Mobutu'. It had to be used instead of the – logical – 'Z' (for 'Zaire') because the latter letter was already 'taken away' by South African orders for Mirage IIICZs and IIIEZs. Similarly, the suffix 'DM' in the designation of Mirage 5DM two-seaters manufactured for Zaire stood for 'Dual Mobutu'.
27 Mamdani, p.85. Mamdani stressed that the Safari Club launched a number of interventions around Africa, the first of which was the one in Shaba, in April 1977. Crucial for related decision-making were the French President Giscard d'Estaing, Egyptian President Anwar el-Sadat, and Moroccan King Hassan II, who also received support from US President Jimmy Carter.
28 George, pp.56, 58, 63-64; Gleijeses, 2002, pp.245-250, 254; Kennes & Larmer, pp.102-116; Junior, 2015 (FAPLA), pp.16, 22, 171-173. Notably, the number of troops the FNLC brought into the fight remains unclear. Contemporary estimates for its troop-strength varied from 2,100 to 6,000, with the author considering the lower range as 'more credible'.
29 For details on the Cuban and MPLA/FAPLA operations in question, see Fontanellaz et all, *War of Intervention, Angola* (Africa@War Volume 31).
30 According to Gleijeses (in 'Truth or Credibility', pp.73-74), the FNLC did request Cuban assistance, but Havana declined. Similarly, while the MPLA in Luanda gave its 'go' signal for both Shaba I and Shaba II, it provided very little direct assistance: indeed, for most of the times it preferred to look the other way while the FNLC was invading Zaire. Unsurprisingly, Ogunbadejo (in 'Conflict in Africa'), stresses that, '...Angola was never deeply involved in the invasion. Not even the American Central Intelligence Agency was able to prove any serious involvement, and it is unlikely that...(it would have) dissipated their forces in an attack on Shaba'.
31 di Malu, pp.27-28.
32 di Malu, p.22.
33 Sonck, 'L'Aermacchi MB 326 Sous le ciel Zairois'.
34 di Malu, pp.29-30. The 3rd Company, 4th Battalion FAZ was commanded by Lieutenant Munanga. It was originally assigned the task of protecting Kolwezi, but then rushed to Sandoa. The night after it arrived in that town, it was abandoned by its commander, Lieutenant Munanga, who returned to Kolwezi for unknown reasons. Munanga was subsequently court-martialled and sentenced to death for cowardice and incompetence.
35 Robin Wright, 'Zaire Rebels seen preparing to open a new Front', Washington Post, 13 April 1977.
36 di Malu, pp.31-33.
37 Ibid, pp.33-34.
38 Delallande, 'Mirage au Congo'.
39 di Malu, p.37.
40 Ibid, p.39. It is at least likely that Djogi imprisoned Ikuku because of the latter's complaints about insufficient provisions for his troops. According to di Malu, Djogi provided only one 45kg sack of rice for 845 troops of the 12th Brigade FAZ upon their arrival at Kamina. Furthermore, he not only prohibited any of Ikuku's officers from entering the officers club at the local military base, but also refused to authorize them quarters: all had to sleep in tents outside – and this during the night when the area was hit by one of typical thunderstorms.
41 Ibid, p.39-41; Flintham, p.112 & Van Nederveen, p.47.
42 Michael T Kaufmann, '2 Captives displayed by Zaire in Stadium: Crowd of 60,000 calls for Death of Men seized in South – They tell of Training by Cubans', *New York Times*, 20 April 1977.
43 Sonck, 'L'Aermacchi MB 326 Sous le ciel Zairois' & di Malu, p.44.
44 'Shaba', *AP*, 25 April 1977 & di Malu, pp.45-46.
45 Sonck, 'L'Aermacchi MB 326 Sous le ciel Zairois'.
46 Ibid. According to Sonck, this was the second MB.326GB of the FAZA lost by that point in time. The first loss occurred at N'Djili IAP in 1976, during a take-off for a training flight, and resulted in the loss of the pilot, Lieutenant Lho.
47 'Zaire condemns two Men with Links to Shaba Invasion', New York Times, 19 August 1977; 'Le Sahara occidental', *Enjeu Maghrébin*, p.304.
48 Van Nederveen, p.47.
49 Nour Bardai (relative to one of Egyptian Mirage-pilots), interview to Tom Cooper, 19 July 2018.
50 Pasierbinski, pp.114-115.
51 di Malu, p.55.
52 According to di Malu (p.55), the invasion force totalled 5,000 FNLC 'regulars'.
53 Sonck, in 'L'Aermacchi MB 326 Sous le ciel Zairois', cites the destruction of five MB.326GBs. For comparison, di Malu cites destruction of four. To compensate for the loss of its MB.326GBs,

the Zairians subsequently placed an order for six MB.326K single-seat fighter jets, and two additional MB.326GBs, while the two Aermacchis damaged at Kolwezi were recovered and sent for repairs to Italy.

54 Pasierbinski, p.116.

55 Van Nederveen, p.48.

56 di Malu, p.57.

57 According to di Malu, the 311th Battalion suffered a loss of 26 men killed and 40 wounded during the entire campaign, indicating that most Western reports about the number of paratroopers killed during that battalion's jump on Kolwezi 'Main' are wildly exaggerated.

58 Kennes, pp.137-138.

59 Odom, Shaba II, p6 & Van Nederveen, p48.

60 Ibid, p.61.

61 Pasierbinski, pp.117-118.

62 While most of the troops of the 2e REP were transported to Zaire on board of UTA's DC-8s, the second echelon of the unit was transferred by transports of the USAF – directly to Lubumbashi.

63 The Belgians proved very reluctant with regards to launching an intervention because their Ministry of Foreign Affairs was negotiating for the release of hostages, via the International Red Cross, with the FNLC's political representatives in Brussels (see Pasierbinksi, pp.115-116).

64 Van Nederveen, p.50.

65 Ironically, once on the ground, the first group of Belgian para-commandos was able to monitor the jump of the 2e REP's second wave.

66 Ibid, p.51.

67 di Malu, p.56.

68 Ibid, pp.68-69.

Acknowledgments

The author would like to thank the following for all the help given when preparing this book:

Tom Cooper – without whom this would simply have been an impossible task – for all his advice and guidance throughout the whole process.

Albert Grandolini for his expert assistance and providing pictures.

Adrien Fontanellaz for help with data on the FNLC, MPLA and the Cubans, plus tips on the Zairian military – simply precious.

Mark Lepko for pictures; Jean Pierre Sonck for help with FAZA research (and who also inspired me years ago when I was publishing Katanga articles in Poland).

Also Andy Miles and Ann Farr from Helion for "polishing" the book to the high standard of the Africa@War series.

Special thanks to Duncan Rogers from Helion for believing in me and, despite many obstacles, supporting me all the way.

This book is dedicated to my son Maksym.

About the author

David Kowalczuk from Poland, is a military history researcher and author, with special interest in post-colonial wars, wars in former Yugoslavia, and Axis collaborators of the World War II. He has published dozens of related articles in the specialized media, World-wide, before narrowing his research to wars in central Africa and southern Europe, lately. This is his first title for Helion's @War series.